JAPANESE LITERATURE

Japanese Literature

An Introduction for Western Readers

By

DONALD KEENE

GROVE PRESS, INC.

NEW YORK

First Grove Press Edition 1955

Sixteenth Printing

Japanese Literature is published in Great Britain by
John Murray in *The Wisdom of the East Series*.

DISTRIBUTED BY RANDOM HOUSE, INC., NEW YORK

GROVE PRESS, INC., 53 EAST 11TH STREET,
NEW YORK, NEW YORK 10003
MANUFACTURED IN THE UNITED STATES OF AMERICA

To
MARY G. DICKINS

CONTENTS

PREFACE

MY intent in writing this little book has been to provide the Western reader—the man who enjoys the great works of the Western literary heritage—with an introduction to some of the things which I have found most beautiful and remarkable in Japanese literature. Since the size of the book was necessarily limited, I had to decide whether to give a bare outline of the long and complex history of Japanese literature, or to select a relatively small number of representative works for fuller discussion. I preferred the latter alternative, even though it meant passing over in complete silence some of the masterpieces most acclaimed by Japanese and Western critics alike ; thus, I was forced to sacrifice any mention of the *Manyōshū*, the most famous collection of Japanese poetry, for it was clear that if I discussed it adequately there would be too little space left for the linked-verse and *haikai*, which greatly appeal to me. The book is thus neither a systematic outline nor a work of reference, but a highly personal appreciation of certain aspects of Japanese literature which I believe to be of especial interest to Western readers.

I have included in the bibliography the titles of histories and other reference works for the guidance of readers who wish to go beyond the scope of this introduction. I have also given a list of readable translations. Thanks mainly to the superlatively good work of Arthur Waley, the Western reader who is ignorant of Japanese need not fear that if this book arouses his curiosity there will be no way to appease it. I have taken advantage of Dr. Waley's kind permission to quote extensively from his writings ; however, all translations which are not specifically acknowledged are my own.

The material of the book, in a somewhat different form, was originally used in lectures delivered at the University of Cambridge during the Lent Term of 1952. The book has since benefited by the helpful suggestions of Mr. J. L. Cranmer-Byng, Mr. E. B. Ceadel and Mr. T. Kamei, to whom I here express my thanks.

I. INTRODUCTION

JAPANESE literature, in spite of its beauty, richness and immediate charm, is as yet inadequately known in the West. The reasons for this neglect are not hard to discover. The intricacies of the Japanese language prevent all but a handful of foreigners from approaching the literature in the original, and the un-inspired nature of many translations often causes the enthusiasm of the most adventurous-minded reader to cool. The good translations which do exist, notably those by Arthur Waley, have won their circle of admirers, but many Western readers remain reluctant to extend their interests in the direction of Japanese literature, if only because of a widespread belief that since the Japanese are a " race of imitators ", their literature can be no more than a pale reflection of the Chinese.

The question of the degree of Japan's indebtedness to China is so basic that I must discuss it briefly, before going on to any more critical consideration of the literature. It would be im-possible to deny the enormous role played by China in the development of Japanese civilization. The method of writing, the philosophy, much of the religion, and certain literary genres had their origin in China, and Japanese have at all times professed the greatest admiration for the older culture, frequently paying it the supreme compliment of imitation. But if this is true of Japan's relationship to China it is equally true of France's and even England's to the classical world, although we do not say of Shakespeare's *Antony and Cleopatra* or of Racine's *Phèdre* that they are " nothing but " imitations. I do not think it fair, either, to say it about those Japanese works which obviously have their roots in China. With the exception of very short periods of indiscriminate borrowing, everything that Japan took from China was filtered through the basically different Japanese temperament and considerably modified. We may contrast this Japanese resistance to the powerful influences of Chinese culture with the almost unquestioning acceptance of them by Korea. Even when the Japanese were trying very hard to take over some Chinese doctrine, such as Confucianism, they appear to have been unable to refrain from altering it ; thus it was that some of the Japanese Confucian scholars were at the same time devout worshippers of the gods of the Land of the Rising Sun and sought to reconcile the two beliefs. The Korean Confucianists, on the other hand, tended towards extreme orthodoxy, and a chance remark attributed to Confucius, that the superior man did not talk while he ate, resulted in centuries of silent meals in Korea, though not in China, much less in Japan.

But Japan has been far more than a skilful modifier of Chinese civilization. In the field of literature, with which we are primarily concerned here, we shall find that Japanese poetry is in most ways unlike Chinese, that the Japanese were writing novels of magnitude and beauty centuries before the Chinese, and that the Japanese theatre, far surpassing the Chinese, ranks with the great dramatic achievements of the world.

It is small wonder that Chinese and Japanese literature are so dissimilar, for the two languages are entirely different. Chinese is a monosyllabic language with musical tones to distinguish the many identical syllables. In its classical form at least, Chinese is a language of great compactness. Japanese, on the other hand, is polysyllabic, has no tones like the Chinese, and sounds rather like Italian, at least to those who do not know Italian. In contrast with the brevity of classical Chinese, Japanese is a language of interminable sentences—sometimes literally

interminable, in which case they are left incomplete, at the end
of the twentieth or fortieth subtle turn of phrase, as if their
authors despaired of ever coming to the end of their task.
Again, Chinese poetry is usually rhymed and is based on a
complicated pattern of musical tones. In Japanese, on the other
hand, rhyme is generally avoided, and the formal rules of
prosody reduce themselves to a matter of counting syllables.
Although the earliest Japanese poems we know, those preserved
in a work of the early eighth century A.D., have lines of irregular
length, the preference for alternating lines of five and seven
syllables soon crystallized among Japanese poets, and this
eventually became the basic rhythm of the language, found
not only in poetry but in almost any type of literary composition.

To give an idea of the appearance of Japanese in transcription
(with the consonants pronounced as in English, and the vowels
as in Italian), I have chosen a passage, ostensibly in prose but
in alternating lines of seven and five syllables. It is one of the
most famous descriptions in the literature, the beginning of the
lovers' suicide journey in the play *Love Suicides at Sonezaki*,
written in 1703 by Chikamatsu. The young man and the
young woman, believing that it is impossible for them to know
happiness together in this life, set out in the early morning for
the wood of Sonezaki, where they are to kill themselves.

Kono yo no nagori	Farewell to this world
Yo mo nagori	And to the night, farewell.
Shini ni yuku mi wo	We who walk the way to death
Tatōreba	To what should we be likened?
Adashi ga hara no	To the frost on the road
Michi no shimo	To the graveyard
Hitoashi zutsu ni	Vanishing with each

Kiete yuku	Step ahead :
Yume no yume koso	This dream of a dream
Aware nare	Is sorrowful.

Are kazōreba	Ah, did you count the bell ?
Akatsuki no	Of the seven strokes
Nanatsu no toki ga	That mark the dawn
Mutsu narite	Six have sounded ;
Nokoru hitotsu ga	The remaining one
Konjō no	Will be for this existence
Kane no hibiki no	The last echo
Kiki osame	We shall hear.
Jakumetsu iraku to	It will echo
Hibiku nari	The bliss of nothingness.

As one may easily see from the above, the sounds of Japanese are very simple. Each syllable generally consists of one consonant followed by one vowel. The restricted number of possible sounds has inevitably meant that there are many homonyms in the language, and countless words contain within themselves other words or parts of words of quite unrelated meanings. For example, the word *shiranami*, meaning " white waves ", or the wake behind a boat, might suggest to a Japanese the word *shiranu*, meaning " unknown ", or *namida*, meaning " tears ". Thus we have blending into one another three ideas, " unknown ", " white waves ", " tears ". One can easily see how from a combination of such images a poem could grow —a boat sails for an unknown destination over the white waves, a lady watches the wake of her lover's boat in tears. From such a multiplicity of word associations evolved the *kake-kotoba*, or " pivot-word ", one of the most distinctive features of Japanese verse. The function of the " pivot-word " is to link two different images by shifting in its own meaning. This may be illustrated by the lines :

> What use are riches when you diamonds,
> Rubies and gold are dross.

In this crude example, " diamond " shifts as it is pronounced from the word " die ", necessary to complete the thought " when you die " to the full meaning of the precious stone, as though the sound " die " started in the poet's subconscious mind a train of images associated with " riches ".

The Japanese " pivot-word " shows a characteristic feature of the language, the compression of many images into a small space, usually by means of puns which expand the overtones of words. In English the use of the pun, or the play on words, for this purpose is not common, but there are examples even before Joyce pushed this method to the extreme with such creations as Meandertalltale. In *Macbeth*, for instance, at a highly tragic moment in the play occur the lines :

> Your castle is surpriz'd ; your wife and Babes
> Savagely slaughtered : To relate the manner
> Were on the Quarry of these murther'd Deere
> To adde the death of you.
>
> (IV, iii, 239–42.)

Shakespeare certainly did not intend the pun on " deer " and " dear " to be greeted with laughter ; it serves rather to increase the complexity of the lines, as it would in a Japanese drama.[1] The great number of similar-sounding words in Japanese affords a perhaps unique range of play on words. Puns were sometimes used for comic effects as in other languages, but the tragic pun

[1] See Muir, Kenneth, " The Uncomic Pun ", in the *Cambridge Journal*, Vol. 3, No. 8, May, 1950.

was also developed, and it was even possible for poets to keep two different sets of images going at the same time through an entire poem without any awkwardness, as in this example :

Kie wabinu, utsurou hito no, aki no iro ni,
mi wo kogarashi no, mori no shita tsuyu.
(SHIN KOKINSHŪ, 1205 A.D.)

One may give two almost entirely different translations of these lines. The first, the more personal interpretation, might be, " Sadly I long for death. My heart tormented to see how he, the inconstant one, is weary of me, I am weak as the forest dew." Or, by using other meanings of the sounds, " See how it melts away, that dew in the wind-swept forest, where the autumn colours are changing ! " Neither of these translations is a full rendering, because in the poet's mind and words there is a constant shifting of the two sets of images, so that the dew which looks as if it soon must be melted away by the autumnal wind becomes one with the woman who has been abandoned by her bored lover, and who wonders what keeps her still alive. It is not that the dew is simply being used metaphorically to describe the woman's state (and to suggest her tears), for the image of the dew is used in its full sense of the natural phenomenon in the second rendering of the poem I gave. The author meant both to be understood at the same time, to draw as it were two concentric circles of meaning, each complete but indissolubly linked to the other.

The effect achieved in this poem was naturally possible only because of the variety of word-play that Japanese affords. But Japanese writers have always been sensitive to the overtones of words, and their exploitation of the possibilities of their language is not merely a fortuitous result of the ease of punning. Place-names and their meanings have especially fascinated the Japanese.

A whole class of early literature consists largely of folk-etymo-
logies of place-names. Most plays contain a journey, as for
example the one quoted above, during which the meaning and
associations of the names of the places passed are used to communicate the emotions of the travellers, whether on their way
to death or to a happy reunion. In the poem about the dew
translated in two such different ways, there is one other image
to be noted : *kogarashi*, which means both " the autumn wind "
and " yearning for ", is the name of a famous forest, and it
may have been from this name itself that the poem had its
genesis, as the poet caught the successive waves of images evoked
by its different meanings.

It would be untrue to infer from this example, however, that
all Japanese poetry is so extremely complicated in its expression.
There are many relatively straightforward poems, and there has
been more than one poet who has decried the artificiality of
the poetry of his time and insisted on the virtues of simple
sincerity. But simplicity and plain expression do not seem to
be truly characteristic of the language, which is surely one of
the world's vaguest yet most suggestive. Japanese sentences are
apt to trail off into thin smoke, their whole meaning tinged
with doubt by the use of little particles at the end, such as
" perhaps ", " may it not be so ? "

The ambiguity in the language is such that at times, especially
in the *Nō* plays, we may have the effect of listening to a string
trio or quartet. There is a total melody which we can recognize,
although we are at the same time aware that it is the combined
product of the individual melodic lines of the several instruments.
Japanese critics, however, have generally been less concerned
with the effects of ambiguity in the language than with the more
deliberate effects of suggestion. Again and again in the history
of literary criticism in Japan we find discussions of the func-

tions of suggestion. Perhaps the most interesting remarks for the modern Western reader are those made by the dramatist Chikamatsu about 1720. In speaking of the art of the puppet theatre, he declared :

"There are some who, believing that pathos is essential to a puppet play, make frequent use of such expressions as 'it was touching' in their writing, or who when chanting the lines do so in voices thick with tears. This is foreign to my style. I take pathos to be entirely a matter of restraint. When all parts of the art are controlled by restraint, the effect is moving, and thus the stronger and firmer the melody and words are, the sadder will be the impression created. For this reason, when one says of something which is sad that it is sad, one loses the implications, and in the end, even the impression of sadness is slight. It is essential that one not say of a thing that 'it is sad', but that it be sad of itself." [1]

It is interesting to note in this connection that over two centuries later the editor of an anthology of English and American imagist poetry made the same discovery as Chikamatsu and wrote : "Poetry is a matter of rendering, not comment. You must not say : 'I am so happy'; you must behave as if you were happy." [2] Imagist poetry was certainly deeply indebted to translations from the Japanese, which perhaps served also to inspire such a critical judgment.[3]

In any case, what was new enough to need saying for Western

[1] Translated in Keene, *The Battles of Coxinga*, p. 95.

[2] Ford Madox Ford in *Imagist Anthology 1930*, p. xiv.

[3] One critic of the imagist school asserted, "Their manifestos are prettily adorned with occult reference to Japanese poetry and criticism, with much expenditure of printer's ink in spelling out exotic-looking syllables in ki, ka and ko." (Quoted in Hughes, *Imagism and the Imagists*, p. 54.)

readers in 1930 had been voiced in one form or another by Japanese authors for centuries. In Japanese literature the unexpressed is as carefully considered as the expressed, as in a Japanese painting the empty spaces are made to have as strong an evocative power as the carefully delineated mountains and pines. There always seems to be an instinctive reluctance to say the obvious words, whether they are " I am so happy " or " It is so sad ". Seldom has it been desired to present the whole of any sight or experience. What the Japanese poets and painters were trying to do instead is perhaps best illustrated by a famous anecdote. It is related how one day a great general, clad in brilliantly polished armour, was waiting for an audience. He was informed that someone was coming who must not see him in armour, and he quickly threw about himself a thin gown of white silk. The effect of the polished armour glinting through the thin silk is the one at which the poets have aimed. To attempt to describe the full magnificence of the general in his armour, or the full beauty of a spring day, has not been the intent of Japanese writers. They have preferred to tell of the glint of the metal, or of the opening of a single blossom, and lead us thus to imagine the rest of the whole from which these few drops have been distilled.

The attempt to represent larger entities by small details resulted in a realism and concreteness in the images which contrast strangely with the misty ambiguity of the general effect. The splash of a frog jumping into the water, the shrill cries of the cicadas, the perfume of an unknown flower, may be the central image around which a Japanese poem is built. In this we may detect the influence of the philosophy of Zen Buddhism which taught, among other things, that enlightenment could come from any sudden perception. The splash of a frog disturbing the ancient stillness of a pond could be as valid a means of

gaining enlightenment as any other, as well as the very embodiment of the movement of life.

It may be seen that the effect of suggesting a whole world by
means of one sharp image is of necessity restricted to shorter verse
forms, and it is in fact in such forms of expression that the
Japanese have in general excelled.   The literature contains some
of the longest novels and plays in the world, some of them of
high literary quality, but the special Japanese talent for exquisite
and suggestive detail has not been matched by a talent for construction.   The earliest novels, if so we may call them, were
often little more than a number of poems and the circumstances
which inspired them.   Such unity as these books possessed came
from the fact that all the poems were credited to one man, or
to one Emperor's court, but no attempt was made to connect
the amorous adventure which gave rise to one verse with the
adventure on the following page.   Even in the later novels
there is no really sharp distinction between the world of poetry
and the world of prose, probably because poetry played a more
common role in Japanese society than it has ever played in ours.
In *The Tale of Genji*, written about 1000 A.D., there are about
800 verses.   Conversations often consist largely of poetry, and
no lover would neglect to send a poem on the day after seeing
his mistress.   But however lovely these poems may be, it cannot
be pretended that they are all essential to the plot of the novel.
Most Japanese novels indeed tend to break up into almost entirely
disconnected incidents in the manner of the old poetry-tales.
In some of the novels there is at least the thread of historical
fact to link the various anecdotes of disparate nature, but in
other works we have digressions of no apparent relevance.
Even in the modern Japanese novel, which has been much
influenced by European examples, we find curiously lyrical
sections floating like clouds over the rest of the work.   For

example, in *The Thin Snow* (*Sasame-yuki* 1946–9) by Tanizaki,
the most important Japanese novel published in the years following the war, there is an exquisite scene in which several of the
principal characters go hunting fireflies of a summer night.
Remembering from old novels and poetry the descriptions of
elegant court ladies in long-sleeved kimonos catching the fireflies
in silken nets, they at first feel disappointed, for they see before
them only a muddy ditch in the open fields. But gradually,
as the insects fill the air with glowing points of light, they are
captured by the beauty so long familiar to them in poetry, and
the description rises to lyrical heights worthy of *The Tale of
Genji*.

If this incident does not advance very greatly the plot of *The
Thin Snow*, nor give us any better understanding of the characters, it is beautiful in itself, and serves in an indefinite but real
way to give us an impression of life in the Japan of 1939, just
as the poetry in *The Tale of Genji* recreates for us the Japan of
950 years before. The digressions in Japanese novels may betray
a weakness in the novelists' powers of construction, but often
their intrinsic beauty is such that our enjoyment of the whole
work is not lessened by the disunity. In retrospect it is as
brilliantly coloured bits somehow merging into an indefinite
whole that we remember the novel. And, as the European
impressionist painters create an illusion of reality in spite of the
fact that their landscapes are composed of seemingly arbitrary
splashes of green, orange, blue, and all the other colours, so the
apparently disconnected incidents of a Japanese novel, blending
into one another, leave us with an imprecise understanding of
their life.

Certain genres of literature have developed to a greater extent
in Japan than in other countries, perhaps as a result of the difficulty
experienced by Japanese writers in organizing their lyrical

impressions and perceptions. These are the diary, the travel account, and the book of random thoughts, works which are relatively formless, although certainly not artless. The charm and refinement of such works may be illustrated by one of the travel accounts, *The Narrow Road of Oku*, by the seventeenth-century poet Bashō. This work begins :

" The months and days are the travellers of eternity. The years that come and go are also voyagers. Those who float away their lives on boats or who grow old leading horses are forever journeying, and their home is wherever their travels take them. Many of the men of old died on the road, and I too for years past have been stirred by the sight of a solitary cloud drifting with the wind to ceaseless thoughts of roaming.

" Last year I spent wandering along the seacoast. In autumn I returned to my cottage on the river and swept away the cobwebs. At last the year drew to its close. When spring came and there was mist in the air, I thought of crossing the barrier of Shirakawa into Oku. Everything I saw suggested travel, and I was so possessed by the gods that there was no controlling my mind. The spirits of the road beckoned, and I found I could do no work at all.

" I patched up my torn trousers and changed the cords on my bamboo hat. To strengthen my legs for the journey I had moxa burned on my shins. Then the thought of the moon at Matsushima began to occupy my thoughts. When I sold my cottage and moved to Sampū's villa, to stay there until I started on my journey, I hung this poem on a post in my hut.

Kusa no to mo	Even a thatched hut
Sumikawaru yo zo	In this changing world may turn
Hina no ie	Into a doll's house.

" When I set out on the 27th March, the dawn sky was misty. Though the pale morning moon had lost its light, Fuji could still be seen faintly. The cherry blossoms on the boughs at Ueno and Yanaka stirred sad thoughts within me, as I wondered when, if ever, I should see them again. My dearest friends had all come to Sampū's house the night before so that they might accompany me on the boat part of the way that morning. When we disembarked at a place called Senju, the thought of parting for so long a journey filled me with sadness. As I stood on the road that was perhaps to separate us forever in this dreamlike existence, I wept tears of farewell.

Yuku haru ya	Spring soon ends—
Tori naki uo no	Birds will weep, while in
Me wa namida	The eyes of fish are tears."

In such works the Japanese have been happiest, able as they are in them to give us their inimitable descriptions of nature, and their delicate emotional responses, without the necessity of a formal plot. A gentle humour and a gentle melancholy fill these pages. This desire to blend images into images, found throughout Japanese poetry, here takes the form of diverse experiences, whether the adventures of a journey, or the day-to-day happenings at the court, blended into the personality of the narrator. There is a general smoothing away of the rough edges of emotion, as something indecorous and rather vulgar. Much is sadly evocative, very little is shattering, either in these books of personal reflections or elsewhere in Japanese literature. Even in the direct imitations by Japanese poets and artists of foreign works, there is always a disinclination to lose the native lightness and grace. The heart-breaking grief experienced by a Chinese poet on seeing the destruction of his city will find its echo in the sweetly nostalgic recollections of his Japanese imitator. Or, the portrait of a Taoist immortal, filled by the Chinese artist with an intense sense of mystery, becomes, in an almost direct Japanese copy, a charming composition of the immortal, his magic toad, pine-trees and clouds.

In this attitude we may find what the Japanese call *miyabi*, literally, " courtliness ", for Japanese literature is prevailingly aristocratic in tone. This does not mean, of course, that there have been no folk ballads, and no novels designed to meet the tastes of the lower classes, but Japanese popular literature has not been of very great importance, at least until recent centuries, and even such works are likely to display far greater elegance than their Western equivalents do. Most of the poetry in the official anthologies was composed by courtiers, and this highly refined art has been so widely disseminated at all levels of society, that the images most likely to come to a peasant-poet's mind today are those first used centuries ago by a prince at the court. There is a difference in this respect between the Chinese and Japanese literary traditions. In China, most of what we think of as literature—love poetry, the drama, the novel, etc.—was considered beneath the dignity of the educated writers, and we possess relatively few works of merit in these genres when compared with the vast bulk of Chinese literature. In Japan, even emperors were not ashamed to write love poetry, and the novels and dramas written by members of the court gave the tone to later works in these forms. But it was not only in the strict sense of having been written by aristocrats that the literature is aristocratic, for we may discover a constant tendency even in the popular literature for it to develop into more refined forms. Again and again we read how some new verse form or theatrical entertainment, originally intended merely as amusement for the lower classes, was purified and codified by persons who saw the

higher, more aristocratic possibilities of the art.   But the elimination of coarseness often means the elimination of vigour as
well, as we can see in the French theatre of the seventeenth
century, and some genres of Japanese literature by choosing not
to offend thereby forfeited the power to interest, becoming no
more than the academic toys of the idle court aristocracy.   The
poet Bashō was aware of this danger, and insisted that the *haiku*,
the short verse form, should aim not only at achieving the
eternally beautiful effects of which all poetry is capable, but
also at creating an impression of freshness.   This was rather an
exceptional attitude, for the earlier masters had preferred to
write " what oft was thought but ne'er so well expressed " rather
than to be original.   Every member of the court was expected
to know by heart the poems in the principal Japanese and Chinese
anthologies, and a slightly different emphasis given to an old
poem would be recognized at once and appreciated as much if
not more than a completely new idea.   The virtuoso approach
to literature, and to art as well, where the artist attempts to do
essentially the same thing as his predecessors but in a slightly
different way, is characteristic of Japan.   The technique may
be illustrated most clearly by the following examples   The first
is a *haiku* by Buson (1716–84) :

> | *Tsurigane ni* | On the temple bell |
> | *Tomarite nemuru* | Resting, asleep |
> | *Kochō ka na* | A butterfly. |

The second example is by Shiki (1867–1902) :

> | *Tsurigane ni* | On the temple bell |
> | *Tomarite hikaru* | Resting, glowing |
> | *Hotaru ka na* | A firefly. |

There is no question here of plagiarism ; rather, Shiki assumed that the persons reading his *haiku* would be familiar with Buson's, and undoubtedly hoped that the new touches which his sensibility imposed on the old poem would be welcomed by a discriminating audience.   Objectively viewed, Shiki's *haiku* is as good as Buson's, although a Western reader would condemn Shiki's as derivative, and his first impulse might be to write a parody of his own, such as " On the temple bell, Resting, chirping, A grasshopper."   Bashō saw the danger of the virtuoso technique practised by the court poets (and by Shiki in the example I have just used), and himself seldom made direct reference to earlier works in his poetry, but he was unable to rid the literature of this characteristic feature.   This is not surprising, for in a country where poetry was recognized by some as a religion it is only natural that the words and images of the old poems come as quickly to a poet's mind as original thoughts, so that he thinks largely in other people's terms, adding only the colouring which is his own.   Similarly, one finds the same stories figuring as the basic plots of every type of Japanese theatrical entertainment.   The audiences which attended a play on one of the familiar themes did not expect to be surprised by the ending nor by any major change in the plot ; it was rather to the details that they looked for the differences resulting from the temperaments of successive dramatists, as in the Greek theatre the story of Oedipus, roughly the same whether treated by Aeschylus, Sophocles or Euripides, nevertheless differed significantly from dramatist to dramatist in the details, as well as in the psychological approach.   In some ways the fact that the subject is prescribed enables the dramatist to display his talents in more subtle ways than in the invention of plot, which may explain why certain dramatists, notably in France, have continued to treat the story of Oedipus, and why Japanese writers of today have not entirely abandoned the traditional themes of their country's literature.

The survival of the old forms would scarcely have been predicted at certain times in the past eighty years when it seemed as though European literature and ideas would overwhelm the native culture. This was especially true during the twenty years immediately following the Meiji Restoration of 1868, a time when Japanese literature reached its lowest point. The university in Tokyo was for a time without a department of Japanese and Chinese literature, while in some schools English but not Japanese literature and history were taught and even the readers used for moral instruction were translations of foreign textbooks.[1] The Minister of Education, who was later assassinated by an opponent of his views, went so far as to favour the use of English instead of Japanese, and one writer even advocated that Japanese men all take European wives so as to improve the size and strength of the race. Such suggestions were not really feasible, but there was a much more serious possibility that the native literature would be entirely eclipsed. Translations of European works soon became the most popular books in Japan. In an attempt to discover the reasons for the success of Western peoples, as shown by their military and commercial achievements, Japanese turned first to books of instruction, such as *Self-Help* by Samuel Smiles, translated in 1870, only two years after the Meiji Restoration, and destined to play an important role in advising Japanese how best to get along in the European manner.

The Western books of a more literary character which were translated in the early days of the new Japan included novels by Bulwer Lytton and Disraeli, and the prevailingly political

[1] Cf. Sansom, *The Western World and Japan*, p. 487. Sansom gives an invaluable account of the whole period.

tone of these works was undoubtedly responsible for the large number of political novels which came to be written in Japan at the time. Japanese critics attempted to evaluate the native literature as they thought Europeans might, and in the search for a Japanese Shakespeare or a Japanese Goethe such writers as the eighteenth-century dramatist Chikamatsu were glorified as never before, while the fame of other writers whose works bore no obvious relationship to the European ideas of literature suffered accordingly. Essays with such titles as " The characters of Chikamatsu's heroines " replaced earlier ones on the importance of literature as a means of encouraging virtue and chastising vice. It was inevitable that Japanese novelists and dramatists should then have begun to write in a revolutionarily different manner. Not only were they interested in aspects of society which had been ignored by their predecessors, but the very language that they used was markedly different. Previous to the Meiji Restoration there had existed a great gap between the colloquial and literary languages. Even the writers of popular romances had used a modified form of the older literary language with its distinctive grammar and vocabulary. But with the large-scale translation of works from English and other European languages it became necessary to make increasing use of the colloquial language in literary expression, for it was found hopelessly awkward to render the conversational approach of the English novel into the flowery patterns of literary-Japanese. The new colloquial style was used not only in translations, but in all works which had been influenced by European example.

There were, it is true, violent protests from various quarters against the adulation accorded to European examples, but although successful in some political and religious matters, such protests failed in so far as literature was concerned. In the past seventy years or more Japanese literature has been intimately affected by all European trends and, in fact, may be regarded in effect as forming a part of the modern movement in Western literature. Ezra Pound included a literary club in Tokyo among the four or five fragments he had shored against his ruins and quoted at length [1] the views of Mr. Katsue Kitasono on the relation between imagery and ideoplasty. Kitasono wrote: " Man has thought out to make a heart-shaped space with two right angles," and Pound commented that this was the " point where the occidental pedlars of imaginary geometries fell down ", indicating that perhaps the Japanese had beaten at their own game their masters in modern literary techniques.

Kitasono otherwise attained some celebrity as a poet of the new style with such verses as

> The boy in the hothouse
> The distant moon
> White flowers
> White.

> A white building
> White
> Pink lady
> White distant view
> Blue sky.

> White boy
> Distant sky
> Hyacinth
> Window
> White landscape.

This was not the most modern of the verses produced in the

[1] In *Guide to Kulchur*, pp. 137–9.

twenties by any means. One, entitled *The White Butterfly*, concluded :

> It is a white butterfly.
> It is a white butterfly.
> It is a white butterfly.
> It is a white butterfly.
> It is a white butterfly.

In spite of such outstanding examples of the new style as *The White Butterfly*, the influence of the West was probably less marked on Japanese poetry than any other branch of literature. Many of the novelists of the new school had already gained fame as translators before publishing their own works, and they reveal at every moment their indebtedness to Western writers, even when the subject is purely Japanese. It is tempting to describe certain novels as being, for example, the "Japanese *Of Human Bondage*" or the "Japanese *Forsyte Saga*", and such names are not devoid of meaning. Even the few novelists who have deliberately affected the old style betray in a thousand ways how much closer they are to the Western novel than to the traditional Japanese one. But the poets have not been so ready to abandon the old forms. Although new styles of poetry were evolved at about the same time for poetry as for the novel and for drama, the best poets continued for the most part to write in the traditional forms, and even works in the new style were likely to fall into the conventional pattern of alternating lines of five and seven syllables, the basic rhythm of the language. The decision of the poets to retain the traditional forms may show that there is a greater conservatism in poetry than in any other genre of literature, or it may represent an awareness that the brief poems were after all the most suited to the language, and more capable of achieving the impressionistic effects sought

by the modern poets than the formless free verse. Certainly
no modern poet has managed to suggest more with so few
words than did Issa (1763–1828) after the death of his only
surviving child. We may imagine that his friends attempted to
console him with the usual remarks on the evanescence of the
things of this world, and the meaninglessness of this existence
as compared to the eternal life in Buddha's Western Paradise.
Issa wrote :

Tsuyu no yo wa	The world of dew
Tsuyu no yo nagara	Is a world of dew and yet,
Sarinagara	And yet.

II. JAPANESE POETRY

ONE of the earliest and most famous statements on Japanese poetry was made in 905 A.D. by Ki no Tsurayuki in his preface to the *Collection of Ancient and Modern Poetry*. This begins :

"Japanese poetry has for its seed the human heart, and grows into countless leaves of words. In this life many things touch men : they seek then to express their feelings by images drawn from what they see or hear. Who among men does not compose poetry on hearing the song of the nightingale among the flowers, or the cries of the frog who lives in the water ? Poetry it is which, without effort, moves heaven and earth, and stirs to pity the invisible demons and gods ; which makes sweet the ties between men and women ; and which can comfort the hearts of fierce warriors."

At first glance these words may seem little more than a conventional statement on the powers of poetry, and indeed there is in Tsurayuki's words more than one suggestion of earlier Chinese remarks. But beneath the smooth rhetorical finish there are some things said, and some unsaid, which are bound to interest the Western reader. First of all, we must note that Tsurayuki claims that poetry has the capacity of affecting supernatural beings, not, as in the West, that the supernatural beings speak through the poet, who is merely an inspired medium for their words. The Japanese may have believed that poetry, like everything else in their country, originated with the gods, but Japanese poets have never turned to a muse or any other divine being for help with their verses. The art, for all the wonderful powers that were attributed to it, was not considered to lie beyond the

unaided talents of man. Tsurayuki listed some of the circumstances under which people have sought consolation in poetry
—" when they looked at the scattered blossoms of a spring
morning ; when they listened of an autumn evening to the
falling of the leaves ; when they sighed over the snow and waves
reflected with each passing year by their looking-glasses ; when
they were startled into thoughts on the brevity of their lives
by seeing the dew on the grass or the foam on the water ; or
when, yesterday all proud and splendid, they have fallen from
fortune into loneliness ; or when, having been dearly loved,
are neglected ''. These remained among the principal subjects
of Japanese poetry and required none of them a muse of fire.

The second point made by Tsurayuki was that poetry helped
as a go-between in love-affairs. This perhaps needs little explana-
tion for Western readers, familiar as we are with the love-poetry
of European languages, but until we read one of the Japanese
court-novels such as *The Tale of Genji*, written about 1000 A.D.,
we are not prepared for the extent to which poetry could be
used for this purpose. Whole conversations between lovers
were carried on in poems, and a skilfully caught poetic allusion
might win a man's heart as easily as a glimpse of his lady's face.
There is a full repertory of Japanese love-poetry, whether protestations of passion, aubades by parting lovers, laments over
faithlessness, or any of the other possibilities in so highly developed a medium. The importance of poetry as a go-between
in love-affairs arose from the to us rather strange manner of
courtship of the Japanese aristocracy in the ninth, tenth and
eleventh centuries, when the techniques of their poetry were
being formulated. Since court ladies might not be seen by any
other men than their recognized husbands, conversations between
lovers, at least in the initial stages, took place with the lady
hidden behind a screen. This formalization of the relations

between the two people favoured the adoption of the more formal language of poetry. When the lovers did not actually speak to one another, they were constantly sending notes back and forth, sometimes tied to sprays of plum-blossom or red maple-leaves, if they happened to be in season. The notes, of course, were also poems, and they were judged not only by their content but by the calligraphy. The usual way a love-affair began was for a young man, who had never seen the lady of his choice, to write her a poem. Then he would wait with impatience for her reply.

"She chose a Chinese paper, very heavily scented. 'Some fault there must be in the stem of this marsh-flower. Else it had not been left unheeded amid the miry meadows by the sea.' Such was her poem. It was written in rather faint ink and Genji, as he eagerly scanned it, thought the hand lacking in force and decision. But there was breeding and distinction in it, more indeed than he had dared to look for ; and on the whole he felt much relieved." [1]

Sometimes, however, the ardent lover had his passion cooled :

"It was an idle repartee, and even the handwriting seemed to Prince Sochi's expectant eye somewhat vague and purposeless. He was, indeed, not at all sure, when he saw it, that he had not made a great mistake." [2]

No better way existed to conquer a lady's heart than with a poem beautifully written on just the right paper. As a final touch :

"She could not but be pleased and flattered by the elegance

[1] *The Tale of Genji* (translated by Waley), one-volume edition, p. 457.
[2] *Ibid.*, p. 497.

of the note ; for it was not only written in an exquisite hand, but was folded with a careless dexterity which she greatly admired." [1]

The writing of love-poetry was not restricted to amorous young people, but was indulged in by all members of the court, from the Emperor down, as a form of literary exercise. In looking through the old anthologies we are apt to find verses like the following one, which is signed simply " A Former Prime Minister ", and entitled *On Hidden Love*.

shirurame ya	Who could detect it ?
ko no ha furishiku	Carpeted with fallen leaves
tani mizu no	A stream in the valley
iwama ni morasu	Trickling between the rocks—
shita no kokoro wo	An all but stifled love.

It should not be supposed, however, that it was only at the court that poetry was considered to be an indispensable accomplishment. Tsurayuki declared that poetry could comfort the hearts of fierce warriors. Indeed, we are likely to be struck when reading Japanese novels, by the composure of heroes in their death struggles who manage to find time to compose a valedictory verse about the falling of the cherry-blossoms, or by the verses of ordinary soldiers who gathered of a winter's night to compose poetry together. But poetry in Japan is the property of all classes of society, and even today almost any Japanese can write a poem without difficulty, although, of course, it may not be of any literary merit. Tsurayuki asked in his preface, " What man does not compose poetry on hearing the song of the nightingale among the flowers ? " and the same question was asked 800 years later by the *haiku* poet Onitsura (1661–1738) :

[1] *Ibid.*, p. 94.

fude toranu	Is there, I wonder,
hito mo arō ka	A man without pen in hand—
kyō no tsuki	The moon tonight !

It remains true to this day that poetry is not felt to be exclusively the business of poets, or even of educated people. This is partially because of the simplicity of Japanese prosody, partially also because the range of the poetry is so limited.

The prosody of Japanese has been determined by the nature of the language. Stress accent, or quantity, the two most common features of European poetry, are ruled out by their absence in Japanese. This is true, of course, of French poetry as well, but the excessive facility of rhyme in Japanese, where every syllable ends in a simple vowel and there are no consonant clusters, deprives the language of this mainstay of French poetry. Japanese verses, then, came to be based on the syllable-count, and different types of poetry are usually distinguished by the number of syllables they contain. Thus, the *tanka* is a poem in 31 syllables, arranged in lines of 5, 7, 5, 7 and 7 syllables. The *haiku*, a more recent development, contains 17 syllables, in three lines of 5, 7 and 5 syllables. In these two forms and in variants based on them is to be found almost all of what Japanese consider to be poetry. As may well be imagined, it is no great problem to compose a verse in only 31 or 17 syllables, without rhyme or metre, but it must be added that it is as difficult in Japanese as in any other language to write anything of value.

The range of the poetry is limited both by the shortness of the verses and also by what it was felt proper to include in a poem. The shortness is responsible, among other things, for the lack of true narrative poetry, since, obviously, very little can be related in 31 syllables, much less 17. But the shortness alone is not accountable for another feature, the rarity of poems of an

intellectual or otherwise non-emotional character. The list
made by Tsurayuki of subjects likely to arouse a man to poetic
expression contains only emotional ones. In contrast, the most
sizeable, if not usually the best parts, of many Chinese poets'
works consist of occasional verse of an almost completely un-
emotional character in any ordinary sense. In Arthur Waley's
book on Po Chü-i, for example, we find such specimens of Po's
lyricism as :

Since the day that old Ho died the sound of recitation has ceased ;
Secretaries have come and secretaries gone, but none of them
    cared for poetry.
Since Ho's day their official journeys have remained unsung ;
The lovely precincts of the head office have waked no verse.
For long I grieved to see you kept in the same humble post ;
I trembled lest the art of high song should sink to its decline.
To-day when I heard of your appointment as Secretary of the
    Water Board
I was far more pleased than when myself I became secretary to
    a Board.[1]

This is an example of the kind of verse which it is impossible
to write in Japanese, and no one would dream of attempting
it. A Japanese political poem is much more likely to take the
form of a wish that the emperor's reign will last until pebbles
become boulders and are covered with moss.

The number of moods in which Japanese poetry can be written
is also limited by tradition. There are few poems written in
burning indignation, like some of the greatest Chinese poetry,
few of religious exaltation, few which touch more than vaguely
on metaphysics or ethics. This list might be prolonged almost

[1] Waley, *The Life and Times of Po Chü-i*, pp. 145–6.

indefinitely until we are left with a very limited variety of subjects considered fit for poetry, and within that limited variety, a limited number of ways of treating them. Most of the verses may be classified as love- or nature-poetry, and the most frequently employed tone is one of gentle melancholy. The falling of the cherry-blossoms and the scattering of the autumn leaves are favourite themes because both of them suggest the passing of time and the brevity of human existence. There is a religious background to such poetry, the type of Buddhism which taught that the things of this world are meaningless and soon faded, and that to rely on them is to put one's faith in dust and ashes. But such religious ideas as are found in Japanese poetry are quite simple, and cannot have disturbed the poets very much. Typically enough, it was the anti-intellectual Zen Buddhism which furnished the only significant religious influence on Japanese poetry.

The uncomplicated nature of the subjects favoured by Japanese poets was perhaps the result of the simplicity of the verse-form, or perhaps it was the simplicity of the ideas which helped to dictate the form. In either case, most Japanese poets did not fret at the narrow limits of the 31-syllable *tanka* ; those who did could write " long-poems " (*nagauta*), although this became an increasingly rare medium, or compose poems in Chinese, as English poets used sometimes to write verse in Latin. For the most part, however, the form and content of traditional Japanese poetry seem perfectly suited to one another, and to correspond with Japanese taste as revealed in other forms of art.

One obvious feature of Japanese poetry, which has been highly praised by critics, is its power of suggestion. A really good poem, and this is especially true of *haiku*, must be completed by the reader. It is for this reason that many of their poems seem curiously passive to us, for the writer does not specify the truth taught him by an experience, nor even in what way it affected him. Thus, for example, the *haiku* by Bashō (1644–94) :

kumo no mine	The peaks of clouds
ikutsu kuzurete	Have crumbled into fragments—
tsuki no yama	The moonlit mountain.

A Western poet would probably have added a personal conclusion, as did D. H. Lawrence in his *Moonrise*, where he tells us that the sight made him " sure that beauty is a thing beyond the grave, that perfect bright experience never falls to nothingness ".   But this is what no Japanese poet would say explicitly ; either his poem suggests it, or it fails.   The verse of Bashō's just quoted has clearly failed if the reader believes that the poet remained impassive before the spectacle he describes.   Even for readers sensitive to the suggestive qualities of the poem, the nature of the truth perceived by Bashō in the sudden apparition of the moonlit mountain will vary considerably.   Indeed, Bashō would have considered the poem faulty, if it suggested only one experience of truth.   What Japanese poets have most often sought is to create with a few words, usually with a few sharp images, the outline of a work whose details must be supplied by the reader, as in a Japanese painting a few strokes of the brush must suggest a whole world.

It is partially because of this feature of suggestion that Japanese poetry is communicated rather inadequately into English.   The Western reader is often in the position of the lover of Russian ballet who watches for the first time the delicate gesture-language of the Balinese dance—no leaps, no arabesques, no entrechats, nothing of the medium with which he is familiar save for the grace and the movement.   The dance—or Japanese poetry—may appear over-refined, wanting in real vigour, monotonous, and to such criticism there is no answer. Their compass will inevitably appear limited to most people, and only the connoisseur will discover areas of suggestion around them.

The word "connoisseur" suggests another difficulty for the Western reader. Japanese poetry, like almost every branch of their arts, is virtuoso in methods, and perfectionist in details. This is in direct contrast with Western poetry, where two or three mediocre stanzas in the middle of a long poem are not considered a serious defect providing that there are a sufficient number of high moments in it. Although the second verses of most of our poems are inferior to the first ones, the cry from the poet's heart or his philosophic perceptions are generally thought worthy of more than a single quatrain. However, the Japanese poet when expressing his feelings is more likely to use a few words of someone of long ago, words as familiar to everyone in Japan as at one time the famous parts of the Bible were familiar in this country, adding a little and giving to these old words the new accent of the present. It is thus possible in a highly concentrated form to express much to the connoisseur familiar with the allusion, and the change from the old poem needs to be very slight if it is expertly managed. Often it is almost impossible to express these slight changes in English translation, so delicate are the variations. If the range of Japanese poetry is small, the shadings within that range can make the English language seem gross and unwieldly.

The problem in translation is accentuated by the fact that there is no poetic correspondence in vocabulary between Japanese and English. For example, Japanese has a rich variety of words for different types of winds, enough to name a whole class of destroyers used in the past war. Or with the word *hanami*, which we may translate "flower-viewing", a poet can suggest gaily-clad crowds enjoying the sight of the cherry-blossoms. Of course we can express the idea in half a dozen words, but the poetic effect is lost.

As a final major difficulty, there is the fact that the overtones of words are not the same. Sometimes this results from the fact that the thing itself is different ; thus, the frog is celebrated in Japan for the beauty of its cries, which are not at all like the croaking with which we are familiar here. But more often it is the poetic tradition which is different. Japanese are never tired of writing about the autumn grasses—all of which have disagreeable Latin names when one attempts to translate—but they seem utterly indifferent, say, to the rose, although familiar with it. This list might be prolonged to cover almost all the most frequent images of both languages.

It must be clear from the above that to appreciate Japanese poetry fully it must be read in the original, but I think that it is possible to communicate some of its qualities by describing the developments in one branch of the poetry. I have chosen the *renga*, or linked-verse, together with the related *haiku*. These in some ways are the most Japanese of verse-forms, and suitable therefore as illustrations.

The linked-verse, in its simplest form, consisted of one *tanka* composed by two people ; that is, one person wrote the first three lines, and the other the last two lines, to make one normal poem. An example of this type of linked-verse may be found even in the *Record of Ancient Matters* (*Kojiki*) of 712 A.D., the oldest surviving Japanese book, but it was not until the eleventh and twelfth centuries that the form became popular. How it happened that one poem came to be divided in two may be seen by comparing the early anthologies with the *New Collection of Ancient and Modern Poetry* (*Shin Kokinshū*) of 1205 A.D. In the earlier poetry there was no fixed place for the break in the verse, which would come at the end of the second, third, or fourth line, but in the *New Collection* it most commonly falls after the third line, as in this poem :

furusato wa	My old home
chiru momijiba ni	Under scattered scarlet leaves
uzumorete	Lies buried now.
noki no shinobu ni	Through the fern by the eaves
akikaze zo fuku	The autumnal winds blow.

MINAMOTO NO TOSHIYORI.

In this example the last two lines of the poem have the effect of a comment on the first three, and almost stand independent. We can see how such a poem might have been created by two people, unlike the older poems which were generally far more of a piece. Linked-verse of a simple kind became in the eleventh and twelfth centuries a popular court pastime. One man would compose the opening three lines, making them as difficult to " cap " as possible, and a second man would demonstrate his virtuosity by supplying the final two lines in spite of the problems. The first major step forward in the development of linked-verse came with the addition of a third verse in three lines of 5, 7 and 5 syllables, thus destroying the limitations imposed by the original *tanka* form of a poem in five lines, and opening the way to poetry chains of many verses of alternating three and two lines. The unit of three verses remained the most important in the long linked-verse, even when the number of links reached 10,000 or more, for each verse had to fit with the one before and the one after. This represented a marked change from the earlier form of linked-verse, where the highest object had been to achieve a brilliant response to a difficult opening. In a long series it was no virtue to compose a verse which it was almost impossible to follow, and thus linked-verse became essentially a co-operative enterprise, and as such was popular

among soldiers, priests and ordinary citizens as well as courtiers,
who found that an evening of linked-verse making was pleasantly
spent.   Generally three or more persons took turns composing
verses, either of 5, 7, and 5 syllables, or of 7 and 7 syllables.
The subject matter of these verses varied from contribution to
contribution, the only requirement being a link of some sort
with the verse immediately preceding.   This is illustrated by
one of the earliest examples of the linked-verse by three people
(from the *Mirror of the Present* of 1170 A.D.) :

Nara no miyako wo	My thoughts go out
omoi koso yare	To the capital at Nara.

FUJIWARA NO KINNORI.

yaezakura	The double-cherry blossoms
aki no momiji ya	And the red leaves of autumn
ika naramu	What are they like ?

MINAMOTO NO ARIHITO.

shigururu tabi ni	With each autumnal shower
iro ya kasanaru	The colours multiply.

ECHIGO NO MENOTO.

Here, the second verse is linked to the first by the fact that
the capital city of Nara was famous for its cherry-blossoms and
bright autumn leaves.   The third verse links to the second in
its reference to the colour of the leaves changing after the
autumnal showers.   But no apparent connection exists between
the first and third verses.   It was, in fact, considered undesirable
to pursue the same subject beyond a few verses.

The existence of a superficially similar type of poetry in China
has led some people to believe that the linked-verse was not
an indigenous Japanese product.   However, a careful examina-
tion of the Chinese *lien-chü*, as it was called, shows that no

connection could have existed between the two types of poetry.
A typical *lien-chü* is this dialogue between one Chia Ch'ung
and his wife, a work of the fourth century A.D. :

Chia : Who is it sighs so sadly in the room ?
Wife : I sigh because I fear our ties may break.
Chia : Our marriage ties are firm cemented ; rocks may
          crumble, but my heart will never change.
Wife : Who does not worry at the end ? 'Tis fate that they
          who meet must part.
Chia : My heart is known to you ; your heart I understand.
Wife : While you are faithful to your word, it's fit I stay
          with you.

This example illustrates two characteristics of the Chinese *lien-
chü*, the unity of subject and the lightheartedness of the tone,
neither at all true of Japanese linked-verse. In any case, I believe
it is clear from what has already been said that the linked-verse
was a natural development in Japanese poetry, and not dependent
on any foreign influence.

The *lien-chü* was never taken seriously by the Chinese, and is
barely mentioned in histories of their literature, but linked-verse
developed steadily in Japan into an extraordinarily complicated
form of poetry, governed by elaborate codes. Of the opening
verse (the *hokku*) it was said, " The *hokku* should not be at
variance with the topography of the place, whether the mountains or the sea dominate, with the flying flowers or falling leaves
of the grasses and trees of the season, with the wind, clouds,
mist, fog, rain, dew, frost, snow, heat, cold or quarter of the
moon. Objects which excite a ready response possess the
greatest interest for inclusion in a *hokku*, such as spring birds
or autumn insects. But the *hokku* is not of merit if it looks as
though it had been previously prepared." The requirements for

the second verse were somewhat less demanding ; it had to be closely related to the first and to end in a noun. The third verse was more independent and ended in a participle ; the fourth had to be " smooth " ; the moon had to occur in a certain verse ; cherry-blossoms could not be mentioned before a certain point ; autumn and spring had to be repeated in at least three but not more than five successive verses, while summer and winter could be dropped after one mention, etc. The rules multiplied to such an extent that one might feel safe in predicting that nothing worthwhile could be written under such handicaps. Yet, although linked-verse increasingly became the toy of dilettanti whose chief accomplishment was exact conformity to the rules, great poetry was occasionally written, especially by Sōgi (1421-1502), the master of the linked-verse.

In 1488 Sōgi and two disciples met at a place called Minase and composed together 100 linked-verses which are considered to be the marvel of the art. The series begins :

> *yuki nagara*   Snow yet remaining
> *yamamoto kasumu*   The mountain slopes are hazy—
> *yūbe ka na*   It is evening.
>
>   Sōgi.
>
> *yuku mizu tōku*   The water distantly flows
> *ume niou sato*   By the plum-scented village.
>
>   Shōhaku.
>
> *kawakaze ni*   In the river-breeze
> *hitomura yanagi*   A cluster of willows—
> *haru miete*   Spring is appearing.
>
>   Sōchō.
>
> *fune sasu oto mo*   The sound of a boat being poled
> *shiruki akegata*   Clear in the clear morning light.
>
>   Sōgi.

There is an effortlessness about these verses which might deceive us into thinking that the rules had been ignored, but verse after verse will be found to be in perfect conformity. The opening one tells us that the season is early spring, when the haze first hovers over the mountains still covered with the winter's snow. The place is indicated as the Minase River by its allusion to this poem by the Emperor Gotoba (1180–1239) :

miwataseba	When I look far out
yamamoto kasumu	The mountain-slopes are hazy
Minase-gawa	Minase River—
yūbe wa aki to	Why did I think that only in autumn
nani omoikemu	The evenings could be lovely ?

And Sōgi tells us that it is evening, thus giving the season, place and time as required. The second verse helps to complete the opening one by continuing the theme of early spring in its mention of the plum-blossoms, the first flowers of the year. It also helps further to identify the setting as the Minase River in its mention of the flowing water, an allusion to another poem on the subject. The third verse also mentions the spring, in keeping with the rule, and continues the water image. The fourth verse breaks the spring image, but continues the water one to three, and also satisfies the requirement of smoothness. There are many other subtleties which it would be difficult to explain here, but the important thing is that in spite of the hampering rules, a poem emerges of surpassing grace and beauty. It is a poem unlike any ever written in the West, as far as I know, in that its only unity is from one verse to the next. Each verse is linked to the one before and the one after, but whereas, for example, the first verse tells us it is evening, the fourth verse is about the early morning ; again, in the sixth verse we are told that autumn is drawing to a close, although the first three

verses have all indicated the season as spring. To give a parallel
in the graphic arts, one may compare the linked-verse with the
Japanese horizontal scroll (*emakimono*). As we unroll one of
the scrolls with our left hand we simultaneously roll up a
correspondingly long section with our right hand. No matter
which segment of the scroll we see at one time, it makes a
beautiful composition, although when we examine it as a whole
it possesses no more unity than a river landscape seen from a
moving boat. Linked-verse at its best produces a somewhat
similar effect.

The raising to so high an artistic level of what had originally
been a kind of parlour game meant that it was necessary for the
fierce warrior who sought comfort in verse, or for any other
amateur poet, to find some newer and simpler verse-form. The
new form which developed in the sixteenth and seventeenth
centuries was the *haikai* or " free " linked-verse. In contrast to
the traditional linked-verse, which had been full of cherry-
blossoms, willows and pale moonlight, the free linked-verse
delighted in mentioning such humble things as weeds, running
noses, and even horse-dung. In time, of course, the new poetic
diction became as stereotyped as the old, but the first result of
the absence of formal rules in the free linked-verse was the
release of floods of linked-verse and of *haiku*, a new form
derived by making an independent unit of the opening verse
of a linked-verse series. It is sometimes also called *hokku*, or
haikai.[1] One man is said to have composed 20,000 verses in a
single day. Obviously the quality of *all* of these verses cannot

[1] Strictly speaking, *haikai* was the general name for the informal type
of poetry exemplified by Bashō and his school ; *hokku* the name of the
opening verse of a linked-verse series ; and *haiku* (a more modern term)
the name given to an independent verse of the *haikai* school. However,
the three words are very often confused.

have been very high, but this expansive, optimistic, and rather vulgar kind of poetry is most characteristic of late seventeenth-century Japan. After long years of internal warfare, the establishment of peace at the beginning of the century had led to a period of great prosperity and a brilliant flowering of the arts. It was natural that Japanese poetry, which had hitherto been marked chiefly by its sobriety and restraint, should become more cheerful and extravagant, and that the shift of the centre of creative activity from the court to the haunts of merchants should be reflected also in the tone. What *is* surprising is that there lived at this time in the capital city of the shoguns a man who is often considered Japan's greatest poet, whose verses are of exquisite refinement, and who himself led so pure a life that he is venerated as a saint by some. This was Bashō (1644–94), the master of the free linked-verse and of the 17-syllable *haiku*, which was its product.

In his conversations with his disciples, Bashō declared that the two principles of his school of poetry were change and permanence. This statement is made more intelligible by a knowledge of the two perils by which Japanese poetry was always menaced. The first of these, and the graver, was staleness and sterility, the result of an excessive study and imitation of earlier masterpieces. Bashō insisted that his style of poetry should "change with every year and be fresh with every month" as he put it. He said, moreover, "I do not seek to follow in the footsteps of the men of old ; I seek the things they sought." That is, he did not wish to imitate the solutions given by the poets of former times to the eternal problems, but sought instead to solve them for himself. This was what he meant by his second principle, that of permanence. When, as under the influence of the new movements in seventeenth-century literature, all traditions were cast aside, and Japanese poets revelled in their freedom, the results were often chaotic. For Bashō both change and permanence had to be present in his *haiku*. In some of his greatest poems we find these elements present, not only in the sense just given, but also, if we may state the terms geometrically, as an expression of the point where the momentary intersects the constant and eternal. We find it, for example, in what was perhaps his most famous *haiku* :

furuike ya	The ancient pond
kawazu tobikomu	A frog leaps in
mizu no oto	The sound of the water.

In the first line, Bashō gives us the eternal component of the poem, the timeless, motionless waters of the pond. The next line gives us the momentary, personified by the movement of the frog. Their intersection is the splash of the water. Formally interpreted, the eternal component is the perception of truth, the subject of countless Japanese poems ; the fresh contribution of Bashō is the use of the frog for its movement, instead of its pleasing cries, the hackneyed poetical image of his predecessors.

If the " perception of truth " is indeed the subject of the poem, we may recognize in it the philosophy of Zen Buddhism, which taught, among other things, that enlightenment was to be gained by a sudden flash of intuition, rather than by the study of learned tomes of theology, or by the strict observance of monastic austerities. When an acolyte enters the Zen priesthood, he is made to sit for long hours in a prescribed position, with his eyes half-closed, and his mind on the Great Nothingness. As he sits there gently swaying, hearing the monotonous incantation of a priest intoning a sutra, and breathing the heavy fragrance of incense, he will suddenly be struck from behind with a light wooden stick, and then, if ever, can occur the flash of enlighten-

ment.   But any sudden perception may lead to this state ; it
was the appearance of the morning star which gave enlightenment to Buddha himself, according to Zen believers.

The images used by Bashō in capturing the moment of truth
were most often visual, as in the *haiku* about the frog, or the
equally famous :

kareeda ni	On the withered branch
karasu no tomarikeri	A crow has alighted—
aki no kure	Nightfall in autumn.

This verse presents so sharp an image that it has often been
painted.   But Bashō did not rely exclusively on visual images ;
the moment might equally well be perceived by one of the
other senses :

shizukasa ya	Such stillness—
iwa ni shimiiru	The cries of the cicadas
semi no koe	Sink into the rocks.

And sometimes the senses were mingled in a surprising modern
way :

umi kurete	The sea darkens,
kamo no koe	The cries of the seagulls
honoka ni shiroshi	Are faintly white.

As these examples indicate, the *haiku*, for all its extreme
brevity, must contain two elements, usually divided by a break
marked by what the Japanese call a " cutting word " (*kireji*).
One of the elements may be the general condition—the end of
autumn, the stillness of the temple grounds, the darkening sea
—and the other the momentary perception.   The nature of the
elements varies, but there should be the two electric poles
between which the spark will leap for the *haiku* to be effective ;

otherwise it is no more than a brief statement. That is the
point which has been missed by such Western imitators of the
haiku form as Amy Lowell, who saw in the *haiku* its brevity
and suggestion, but did not understand the methods by which
the effects were achieved. Here are two of Miss Lowell's *haiku* :

A Lover

If I could catch the green lantern of the firefly
I could see to write you a letter.

To a Husband

Brighter than the fireflies upon the Uji River
Are your words in the dark, Beloved.[1]

In these examples the words are poetic, but the verses do not
have the quality of a *haiku*, for the reason I have given. They
suggest rather the shorter links of 14 syllables in a linked-verse
series, which, however, never stand alone, and cannot be considered complete poems. There is an art to writing these shorter
links as well, and although Bashō today is famed chiefly for his
haiku in 17 syllables, he was also a master of the 14-syllable link.
As I have mentioned, the *haiku* itself originated as the opening
verse of a linked-verse series, and it in fact never lost the poten-
tiality of serving as a poetic building block. Thus, to Bashō's
haiku, " The ancient pond, a frog jumps in, the sound of the
water ", his disciple Kikaku added a link in 14 syllables :

ashi no wakaba ni	On the young shoots of the reeds
kakaru kumo no su	A spider's web suspended.

This link fulfils the purpose of complementing the opening one.

---

[1] From *Pictures of the Floating World*. Miss Lowell's best *haiku* are
probably the ones on modern themes in *What's O'Clock* ?

In the mention of the young shoots it tells us that the season
is mid-spring, not specified by Bashō, and in the image of the
spider's web strengthens the impression of stillness suggested by
the words " the ancient pond ". But, as we might expect, it
was Bashō himself who composed the second verse, which is
generally considered the model of its kind. His pupil Kakei
had given the opening verse :

> shimotsuki ya   November—
> kō no tsukuzuku   The storks tentatively
> narabi ite   Standing in a row.

To this Bashō added :

> fuyu no asahi no   The winter sunrise
> aware narikeri   So touching a sight.

In adding this link Bashō not only supplied a new image of
his own, but greatly increased the effectiveness of the opening
verse. The red winter's sun, rising over the landscape, casts
its harsh light on the miserable little flock of storks, uncertainly
standing in the cold. If it had been said directly of the storks
that they were a " touching sight ", it would have killed the
suggestion of the image, but the unexpectedness of referring
to the sunrise as " touching " gives freshness and force to the
statement, and the unspoken comparison is left to the reader.

It may be wondered how often it was possible to assemble a
group of linked-verse enthusiasts capable of producing a series
of real merit. It cannot have been very often. Bashō, in his
travel diary, *The Narrow Road of Oku*, gives us the circumstances
of one series :

" As it was our plan to sail down the Mogami River, we
waited at a place called Ōishida for the weather to clear. The

seeds of the old school of *haikai* had been scattered here, and
the days of its flowering, unforgotten, still brought the sound
of the northern flute to the solitary lives of the poets of
Ōishida. They said, ' We are groping ahead on the road of
poetry, uncertain as to whether to follow the old or the new
way, but here no one can guide us. Will you not help ? '
I was unable to refuse them, and joined in making a roll of
linked-verse. Of all the poetry-gatherings of my journey,
this showed the most taste.''

We may imagine the effort put forth by the local poets to be
worthy of the honour of joining with the great master, and they
did not do badly. Bashō began the series with :

samidare wo	Gathering seawards
atsumete suzushi	The rains of May, coolly flows
Mogami-gawa	Mogami River.
kishi ni hotaru wo	The little fishing boats tie
tsunagu funagai	Their firefly lights to the bank.
	ICHIEI.
uribatake	The melon fields
izayou sora ni	Wait for the moon to shine from
kage machite	The hesitant sky.
	SORA.
sato wo mukai ni	Going off towards the village
kuwa no hosomichi	A path through the mulberry-trees.
	SENSUI.

These verses have charm and blend with one another suitably
to describe scenes in Ōishida during the spring rains. But often,
even when Bashō himself was taking part, the linked-verse
tended to break up into unrelated fragments, and one has the
impression then that the participants are more anxious to express

their happy thoughts than to fit links into a poetic chain. This may be illustrated by the beginning of another series :

tsutsumi kanete	The wintry shower
tsuki toriotosu	Unable to hide the moon
shigure ka na	Lets it slip from its grasp.

TOKOKU.

kōri fumiyuku	As I step over the ice
mizu no inazuma	Lightning flashes in the water.

JŪGO.

shida no ha wo	The early huntsmen
hatsu karibito no	Tie fronds of the white fern
ya ni oite	To their arrows.

YASUI.

kita no mikado wo	Pushing open the northern
oshiake no haru	Palace gates—the spring !

BASHŌ.

bafun kaku	Above the rakes
ōgi ni kaze no	For sweeping horse-dung, the air
uchikasumu	Appears hazy.

KAKEI.

This is unhappily a more representative example of linked-verse making than any I have given thus far since, in the nature of things, it was almost impossible to produce a really successful series. Here, some of the links have great individual merit, but the connections between them are poor. Thus, the image of the lightning flashes, a characterization of the familiar jagged white patterns left around footprints in the ice, is made the more brilliant by the overtones of the sharp sound of the cracking ice, and the apprehension aroused in the walker, like that on hearing thunder. But the verse has unfortunately nothing to do with

the case, as far as the total poem is concerned.   The next three
verses are ostensibly linked because they all treat of early spring ;
it is then that the hunters decorate their arrows with fern, and
then, too, that a haze appears in the air—although the conceit
of having the fumes of the horse-dung called haze certainly
does not come off so successfully as the lightning image.   If one
recalls the effortless flowing beauty of the poetry composed at
Minase, these carefully contrived bits hardly seem to be worthy
of the name of linked-verse.   It is small wonder, then, that
this form of poetry gradually died out.   For linked-verse to
be as successful as those made at Minase, it was necessary for
at least three poets of exceptional talents to join efforts, and to
try, in so far as possible, to subordinate every other consideration
to the perfection of the whole.   We are reminded in this of a
string quartet, where the music can as easily be spoiled by the
ostentatious virtuosity of one member as by the incompetence
of another.   The man who composed the verse about the lightning flash was thinking mainly of creating an effect with his
brilliant image ; a true master of linked-verse would have fore-
gone this pleasure in favour of the harmony of the entire series.
At its best the linked-verse was a unique medium for the expression of the successive images evoked in the minds of different
poets, a multiple stream of poetic consciousness, as it were,
producing an effect akin to music.   The fact that it lacks the
formal structure of more conventional kinds of poetry was of
help to the Japanese, who have never been strong on the construction of poetry or prose, and who were enabled by the
linked-verse to extend their lyricism beyond the brief compass
of a *tanka* or *haiku* without danger of formlessness.   That is,
as long as each verse fitted securely into the next, and the poetry
was maintained at a high evocative level, there was no need for
a carefully worked-out beginning, middle and end, a develop-

ment and a climax, or any such requirement. But when the art of properly fitting the verses was lost, linked-verse dropped immediately to what it had been at its inception, a parlour game, and as such was abandoned by the important Japanese poets. Such men as Issa (1763–1828) preferred to devote their energies to the *haiku*, which became and has remained the favourite poetic form of the Japanese people.

It was the *haiku* also which first attracted the attention of Western poets, particularly those of the imagist school. Almost all the poets represented in the first imagist anthology were fascinated by the miniature Japanese verses with their sharp evocative images, and some composed imitations.[1] Richard Aldington tells how

> One frosty night when the guns were still
> I leaned against the trench
> Making for myself hokku
> Of the moon and flowers and of the snow.[2]

Slim volumes with such revealing titles as *Pictures of the Floating World* and *Japanese Prints* indicate how congenial these poets found the *haiku*, and, although the main thesis of this school, that poetic ideas are best expressed by the rendering of concrete images rather than by comments, need not have been learned from Japanese poetry, it is hard to think of any other poetic literature which so completely incarnates this view.

[1] F. S. Flint wrote in 1915 about the origins of the imagist school of poetry, " I think that what brought the real nucleus of this group together was a dissatisfaction with English poetry as it was then (and is still, alas !) being written. We proposed at various times to replace it by pure *vers libre* ; by the Japanese *tanka* and *haikai* ; we all wrote dozens of the latter as an amusement." (Quoted in Hughes, *Imagism*, p. 11.)

[2] *The Complete Poems of Richard Aldington*, p. 86.

III. THE JAPANESE THEATRE

THE drama is the branch of Japanese literature which has attracted the widest attention in the West, meriting the praise it has won by its beauty and by a diversity scarcely to be matched in any other country. At least four major types of theatrical entertainment exist today : the *Nō*, with a repertory chiefly of fourteenth- and fifteenth-century plays ; the puppet theatre, for which Japan's most celebrated dramatists wrote in the seventeenth and eighteenth centuries ; the *kabuki*, or lyrical drama, which was the popular theatre from the seventeenth century to recent times ; and, finally, the modern drama, written at first largely under Western influence, but now independent, and possessing considerable merit.

Of these four types of theatre, the *Nō* has most interested Western readers, largely as a result of the translations of Ezra Pound and Arthur Waley. It was to the *Nō* that the poet Yeats turned about 1915 for a form of drama " distinguished, indirect and symbolic ", as he put it, and the continued interest in the *Nō* is reflected by performances during recent years in Paris and Berlin. But before discussing those qualities in the *Nō* which have most appealed to Western readers and audiences, some word must be said about the history of this dramatic form.

The name *Nō* itself means " talent ", and by a derived association, the exhibition of talent, or a performance. It was not by this name, however, that the theatre was generally called until recent times. Previously, this most aristocratic of theatrical mediums was known as *sarugaku*, or " monkey-music ", a name perhaps indicative of its origins. The earliest mentions of this " monkey-music " show that it was a lively mixture of song and

dance combined with a certain amount of miming. Some
people believe that there was Chinese influence in the naming
of this entertainment, if not in its form as well, but the early
" monkey-music " was of so elementary a nature that it is
almost impossible to prove whether or not it underwent foreign
influence. Performances under this name go back at least as
far as the tenth century A.D., and there no doubt were similar
forms of entertainment for many years previous. There was also
a rival school of theatrical performances called *dengaku*, or " field-
music ", which flourished especially in the thirteenth and fourteenth centuries, and which seems to have had its origins in the
festivities attending harvest celebrations and other agricultural
holidays. " Field-music " came to be associated with various
shrines and consisted of elaborate programmes of dancing and
singing, together with playlets acted by the dancers. Our
knowledge of the theatre of the thirteenth century and before
is so imperfect that we are unable to ascertain just what relationship existed between the " monkey-music " and the " field-
music ", and in fact it is often difficult to distinguish the two,
for both came to be performances of much the same nature.
What is perhaps most significant is that the *Nō* drama, in spite
of its later themes, was apparently of secular origin, although
it undoubtedly underwent some religious influence through the
" field-music " and other dramatic forms.

By the middle of the fourteenth century the *Nō* had assumed
much of its present shape ; that is, it was a combination of
singing, dancing and music, differing from earlier dramatic forms
chiefly in that it had plots which unified the three elements.
By the end of the same century this rather simple entertainment
had been lifted to its highest powers of expression by two men :
Kanami Kiyotsugu (1333–84) and his son Seami (or Zeami)
Motokiyo (1363–1443). The *Nō* play, as it took final form

in their hands, had a principal dancer (or protagonist), and assistant (or deuteragonist), and various accompanying personages, usually not more than four or five actors in all, plus a chorus. The texts of the individual plays are short, generally not even so long as a single act of a normal Western play, but the singing and dancing made them take about an hour to perform. I think that the best introduction to the technique of a *Nō* play is the brilliant pastiche of one written by Arthur Waley on the subject of the *Duchess of Malfi*.

" The persons need not be more than two—the Pilgrim, who will act the part of the *waki* [or deuteragonist], and the Duchess, who will be *shite* or Protagonist. The chorus takes no part in the action, but speaks for the *shite* while she is miming the more engrossing parts of her role.

" The Pilgrim comes on to the stage . . . and then names himself to the audience thus (in prose) :

" ' I am a pilgrim from Rome. I have visited all the other shrines of Italy but have never been to Loretto. I will journey once to the shrine of Loretto.'

" Then follows (in verse) the *Song of Travel* in which the Pilgrim describes the scenes through which he passes on the way to the shrine. While he is kneeling at the shrine, the Protagonist comes on to the stage. She is a young woman dressed, ' contrary to the Italian fashion ', in a loose bodied gown. She carries in her hand an unripe apricot. She calls to the Pilgrim and engages him in conversation. He asks her if it were not at this shrine that the Duchess of Malfi took refuge. The young woman answers with a kind of eager exaltation, her words gradually rising from prose to poetry. She tells the story of the Duchess's flight, adding certain intimate touches which force the priest to ask abruptly, ' Who is it that is speaking to me ? ' And the girl, shuddering (for it is hateful to a ghost to name itself), answers : ' *Hazukashi ya !* I am the soul of the Duke Ferdinand's sister, she that was once called Duchess of Malfi. Love still ties my soul to the earth. Pray for me, oh, pray for my release ! '

" Here closes the first part of the play. In the second the young ghost, her memory quickened by the Pilgrim's prayers . . . endures again the memory of her final hours. She mimes the action of kissing the hand, finds it very cold. And each successive scene of the torture is so vividly mimed that though it exists only in the Protagonist's brain, it is as real to the audience as if the figure of dead Antonio lay propped upon the stage, or as if the madmen were actually leaping and screaming before them. Finally she acts the scene of her own execution :

> Heaven-gates are not so highly arched
> As princes' palaces ; they that enter there
> Must go upon their knees. (*She kneels.*)
> Come, violent death,
> Serve for mandragora to make me sleep !
> Go tell my brothers, when I am laid out,
> They then may feed in quiet.
> 　　　　(*She sinks her head and folds her hands.*)

" The chorus, taking up the word ' quiet ', chant a phrase from the Lotus Sutra, ' In the Three Worlds there is no quietness or rest '. But the Pilgrim's prayers have been answered. Her soul has broken its bonds ; is free to depart. The ghost recedes, grows dimmer and dimmer till at last it vanishes from sight." [1]

[1] Waley, *The Nō Plays of Japan*, pp. 53-4.

In many respects the Nō resembled the Greek drama. First of all, there was the combination of text, music and dance. Secondly, both theatres used a chorus, although in the Nō the chorus never takes any part in the action, confining itself to recitations for the principal dancer when he is in the midst of his dance. Again, the Nō uses masks, as did the Greek drama, but their use is restricted to the principal dancer and his companions, especially when they take the parts of women. Mask-carving has been considered an important art in Japan, and together with the gorgeous costumes, the masks add much to the visual beauty of the Nō. In contrast, the scenery is barely sketched, consisting usually of no more than an impressionistic rendering of the main outlines of the objects portrayed. The music, at least to a Western listener, is not of great distinction, very rarely rising to the level of melody, and most often little more than an accentuation of the declaimed or intoned word. A flute is played at important moments in the play, and there are several drums, some of which can serve to heighten the tension of the audience. The actual theatres in which the Nō plays are performed are small. Their most striking features are the *hashigakari*, a raised passage-way leading from the actors' dressing-room through the audience to the stage, and the square, polished-wood stage itself. The audience sits on three, or sometimes only two, sides of the stage, which is covered by a roof of its own like that of a temple. The actors make their entrances through the audience, but above them, and pronounce their first words before reaching the stage, an extremely effective way of introducing a character.

The performances in a Nō theatre last about six hours. Five Nō plays are presented in a programme, arranged as established in the sixteenth century. The first play is about the gods, the second about a warrior, the third about a woman, the fourth about a mad person, and the final play about devils, or sometimes a festive piece. Each of the plays in the Nō repertory is classified into one of these groups, and the purpose of having this fixed programme is to achieve the effect of an artistic whole, with an introduction, development and climax. The third, or woman-play, is the most popular, but to present a whole programme of such plays would mar the total effect as much, say, as having an Italian opera with five mad scenes sung by successive coloratura sopranos.

The tone of the Nō plays is serious, and often tragic. To relieve the atmosphere, the custom arose of having farces per-formed in between the Nō dramas of a programme, often parodies of the pieces that they follow. It might be imagined that the alternation of mood from the tragic tone of the Nō to a broad farce and then back again would prove too great a wrench for the sensibilities of the audience. This is not merely a case of comic relief in the manner of Shakespeare, for the farces last almost as long as the serious parts, and often specifically deride them. But the Japanese audiences have apparently enjoyed the very sharpness of the contrast between the two moods.

On the whole, however, the humour of the Japanese farces is not very interesting to us, and when a Western reader thinks of the Nō theatre, it will be of the tragedies. What are the qualities most to be admired in these works ? There is first of all the poetry. This is written in alternating lines of 7 and 5 syllables, like most other Japanese verse, but in the plays attains heights otherwise unknown in the language. The short verses are sometimes miracles of suggestion and sharp imagery, but, at least for a Western reader, lack the sustained power of the greatest poetry. The Nō provides a superb framework for a dramatic poet. It is in some ways an enlarged equivalent of the

tiny *haiku*, portraying only the moments of greatest intensity
so as to suggest the rest of the drama. Like the *haiku* also, the
Nō has two elements, the interval between the first and second
appearance of the principal dancer serving the function of the
break in the *haiku*, and the audience having to supply the link
between the two. Sometimes there is also the intersection of
the momentary and the timeless which may be noted in
many *haiku*. Thus, for example, in the first part of the play
Kumasaka, a travelling priest meets the ghost of the robber
Kumasaka, who asks him to pray for the spirit of a person whom
he will not name. Later that night the priest sees the robber
as he was in former days, and the robber rehearses the circumstances of his death in impassioned verse, ending :

" Oh, help me to be born to happiness."
    (*Kumasaka entreats the Priest with folded hands.*)
The cocks are crowing. A whiteness glimmers over the night.
He has hidden under the shadow of the pine-trees of Akasaka,
    (*Kumasaka hides his face with his left sleeve.*)
Under the shadow of the pine-trees he has hidden himself away.[1]

In this play the meeting of the priest and robber is fortuitous,
the happening of a moment, but the desperate struggle of the
robber to escape from his past into the path of salvation goes
on and on.

Behind these plays, as behind the *haiku*, were the teachings
of Zen Buddhism, whose greatest influence is probably found
in the form of the Nō itself—the bareness of the lines of the
drama, and the simplicity of the stage and sets. These teachings,
which inspired so much of Japanese literature and art in the
fourteenth and fifteenth centuries, probably came to the Nō
largely with Kanami and Seami, who were closely associated

[1] Waley, *The Nō Plays of Japan*, p. 101.

with the court of the shoguns, which was deeply influenced by Zen masters. The use of Zen ideas takes various forms in the plays. In most of them the secondary character (the *waki*) is a priest, and sometimes he uses the language and ideas of Zen Buddhism. In the play *Sotoba Komachi*, one of the greatest, it is the poetess Komachi who voices the Zen doctrines, rather than the priests. She declares, confounding them :

> " Nothing is real.
> Between Buddha and Man
> Is no distinction, but a seeming of difference planned
> For the welfare of the humble, the ill-instructed,
> Whom he has vowed to save.
> Sin itself may be the ladder of salvation."
>
> (*Chorus*) So she spoke, eagerly ; and the priests,
> " A saint, a saint is this decrepit, outcast soul."
> And bending their heads to the ground,
> Three times did homage before her.[1]

The same play contains some of the most beautiful lines of the entire body of Nō plays. This is the story of the poetess Komachi, who when young was noted for her beauty and for the cruelty she showed to her lovers. In the play she is a hag, abandoned by the world, who suffers for her cruelty of former days. The chorus recites of her :

> The cup she held at the feast
> Like gentle moonlight dropped its glint on her sleeve.
> Oh how fell she from splendour,
> How came the white of winter
> To crown her head ?
> Where are gone the lovely locks, double-twined,

[1] Waley, *The Nō Plays of Japan*, p. 155.

The coils of jet?
Lank whisps, scant curls wither now
On wilted flesh ;
And twin-arches, moth-brows tinge no more
With the hue of far hills. " Oh cover, cover
From the creeping light of dawn
Silted seaweed locks that of a hundred years
Lack now but one.
Oh hide me from my shame." [1]

It is such poetry as this, and the hard and formal structure
of the plots, which have most attracted Western readers to the
Nō. Yeats, in explaining why he had adopted the form of the
Nō for his series of plays on Irish legends, declared, " It is natural
that I go to Asia for a stage-convention, for more formal faces,
for a chorus that has no part in the action . . . A mask will
enable me to substitute for the face of some commonplace player
. . . the fine invention of a sculptor. A mask . . . no matter
how close you go is still a work of art . . . and we shall not
lose by staying the movement of the features, for deep feeling
is expressed by a movement of the whole body." [2] In the
poetry itself, as revealed to him in translation, Yeats discovered
patterns of symbols which also attracted him greatly. But not
even in Waley's fine translations can the full power of the poetry
of the Nō be revealed, and judgments on its quality must be
based on the originals.

In the styles used in the Nō plays we have another parallel
with the Greek theatre. There is a marked difference in the
language of quiet and emotionally important scenes, a difference
like that between the iambics and the choral songs of a Greek

---

[1] *Ibid.*, pp. 156–7.
[2] Yeats, introduction to *Certain Noble Plays of Japan*, p. vii.

drama.   The quiet scenes are in prose which must have been
very close to the colloquial of the time, but the poetry of the
sung parts is of extraordinary complexity and difficulty.   It
abounds in allusions and puns, and especially in the *kake-
kotoba* or "pivot-words" already discussed above.[1]   As an
example of the poetry of a *Nō* play, we may consider a short
passage from *Matsukaze*, written by Kanami and revised by
Seami.   This is the story of two fisher-girls, Matsukaze and
Murasame, who long ago in the past were befriended by a
nobleman banished to their lonely shore.   In the first part of
the play a travelling priest asks shelter at their house after seeing
them dip water from the sea.   He discovers their identities, and,
in the second part, Matsukaze, the chief dancer, appearing in
the hunting-cloak left behind by the nobleman, enacts their
story.   During one part of her dance the chorus recites for her:

okifushi wakade	Awake or asleep,
makura yori	From my pillow
ato yori koi no	And in my footsteps
semekureba	Love pursues me.
semukata namida ni	Helpless, in tears
fushi shizumu	I fall and sink
koto zo kanashiki	O sorrowful.

This passage depends for its full effect on the recognition of
an allusion and on a "pivot-word".   The allusion is to a poem
in the *Collection of Ancient and Modern Poetry* of 905 A.D. :

makura yori	From my pillow
ato yori koi no	And from the foot of the bed
semekureba	Love comes pursuing.
semu kata nami zo	What am I to do?
tokonaka ni oru	I'll stay in the middle of the bed.

[1] See above, p. 5.

The allusion to this gay poem in a moment of extreme distress is a psychologically effective device ; a similar use of incongruous poetry is found in Ophelia's mad scene, and, in our own day, in *The Waste Land*, where Eliot quotes Ophelia's "good night, ladies, good night, sweet ladies, good night, good night", after a sordid lower-class scene.

The " pivot-word " in the passage I have cited is one of the best, a splendid example of the use of this device.   The words *semukata nami* mean " helpless " ; by addition of the syllable " da ", we got the word *namida*, " tears ".   Thus the bridge is made between the helplessness of the girl and her tears, the meaning shifting imperceptibly from one image to the other.

It may be wondered to what degree such passages were intelligible to the audience.   Arthur Waley has contended that general familiarity with the old poems, especially in the form of songs, must have made comprehension far more general than we might suppose.   Nevertheless, it is true that the *Nō* increasingly became the pastime of the court aristocracy, the group best trained in recognizing poetic allusions and feats of verbal dexterity.   The middle and lower classes had to wait until the end of the sixteenth century for forms of theatrical entertainment which were designed primarily for their tastes. .These new forms included the *kabuki*, a brilliant dramatic, but essentially not a literary, art, and the *jōruri*, or puppet theatre, in my opinion a far more important literary medium.   Japan is far from being the only country in which the puppet theatre has a long history, but elsewhere it is seldom considered a very exalted form of art.   The puppet-plays produced in Europe are usually either adaptations of plays originally written for actors, or else are trifles calculated to delight or amuse by their ingenuity. In Japan the puppet theatre has been a serious medium for creative artists ; in fact, the greatest Japanese dramatist,

Chikamatsu (1653–1725), wrote all of his famous plays for the puppets, and even today, when this theatre has fallen rather out of public favour, it remains at an artistic level probably unequalled by the theatre of living actors.

The *jōruri* would have been impossible without the *Nō* before it, even though the methods of the two are in some ways so dissimilar. The tradition of masks made it easier for audiences to accept the expressionless faces of the puppets, and the chorus reciting for a *Nō* dancer led the way to a chanter delivering lines for voiceless puppets. Indeed, in its early days the *jōruri* was not only easier to understand, but more realistic than the *Nō*, in spite of the fact that the puppets were rather crudely made. This is indicated by the account we possess of a performance of 1647. A philosopher visited a theatre where he saw wooden puppets dressed as " men, women, monks or laity, immortals, soldiers, horsemen and porters. There were dancers and musicians who beat time with fans and drums. Some leapt about and some rowed boats and sang. Some had been killed in battle, and their heads and bodies were separated. Some were dressed in the clothes of the gentry. Some shot arrows, some waved sticks, and some raised flags or bore aloft parasols. There were dragons, snakes, birds, and foxes that carried fire in their tails, at which all the spectators marvelled. . . . The puppets were just as if they were alive." [1] Certainly this performance sounds more lively than a *Nō* tragedy, with its gloomy poetry and slowly executed dancing. The tricks of the puppet-operator, such as having fire in the foxes' tails as in Japanese ghost stories, were undoubtedly meant to capture the interest of the audience by their realism. The philosopher declared that the puppets seemed to be alive. However, although such facile realism undoubtedly appealed to the audiences, it was rejected

[1] Quoted in Keene, *The Battles of Coxinga*, p. 20.

by all the men who contributed importantly to the advance of the art of the puppet theatre, and the history of the development of this art might almost be made in terms of steps away from realism. Take, for instance, the technique of handling the puppets. At first the operators were hidden in such a way that the audience could see only the puppets, which were either manipulated by strings from above, like our marionettes, or, more commonly, held up from below by an operator with his hands inside the puppet's body. The chanter was also concealed, to increase the illusion that it was the puppet who was acting and talking by himself. As time went on, however, the size of the puppets increased until they were about two-thirds that of the operators, and various developments made it necessary for three men to work each of the important puppet figures. This they did in full view of the audience. The chanter also emerged from his place of concealment. When we see pictures of the puppet theatre with the three men clad in bright or sombre costumes standing beside each puppet and the row of musicians seated to the side, it seems impossible that any semblance of dramatic illusion could be preserved. Why, we may wonder, did a great dramatist like Chikamatsu, who had already written successful plays for actors, choose this unlikely form, and why did the Japanese public, for at least a century, find the puppet theatre more enjoyable than any other ? The answer may be found in the fact that although in Europe the attempt has been to make puppets seem as lifelike as possible, in Japan actors to this day imitate the movements of puppets. It was only by turning its back on realism, as the Nō before it had also done, that the puppet theatre could achieve its high dramatic purpose. The best European marionettes are almost human. This means that the more proficient the operators get the less point there is in having marionettes, except as a pure exercise in manual

dexterity.   In depriving the marionettes of their unreality, they
forfeit every artistic possibility.   As Yeats said, " all imaginative
art keeps at a distance, and this distance once chosen must be
firmly held against a pushing world"   This is the secret of the
Nō and the puppet theatre.   By keeping us at a distance from
the stage the Japanese dramatists admit us to their special domain
of art.   What the puppet theatre can mean to a sensitive Western
observer, is revealed by this statement of the French poet Paul
Claudel : " The living actor, whatever his talent may be, always
bothers us by admixing a foreign element into the part that he
is playing, something ephemeral and commonplace ; he remains
always a man in disguise.   The marionette, on the other hand,
has no other life or movement but that which it draws from the
action.   It comes to life with the story.   It is like a shadow that
one resuscitates by describing to it all it has done, which little
by little from a memory becomes a presence.   It is not an actor
who is speaking ; it is a word which acts.   The creature made
of wood is the embodiment of the words spoken for it. . . . By
other means the jōruri arrives at the same result as the Nō." [1]
   It is not really to be wondered at, in view of the effect Claudel
describes, that Chikamatsu preferred to write for the puppet
theatre.   It appears that he wanted first of all a dramatic form
which would free him from the liberties taken with his texts
by actors, who regarded their parts merely as vehicles for the
exhibition of their special talents.   His understanding of the
potentialities of the puppet stage convinced him that he could
better entrust his plays to dolls than to human beings.   But
Chikamatsu was well aware that the puppet theatre required
a special type of writing.   He said, " Jōruri differs from other
forms of fiction in that, since it has primarily to do with puppets,

[1] Claudel, introduction to Contribution à l'Etude du Théâtre des Poupées,
pp. xii–xiv. (Quoted in Keene, p. 93.)

the texts must be alive and filled with action. Because *jōruri* is performed in theatres that operate in close competition with those of the *kabuki*, which is the art of living actors, the author must impart to lifeless wooden puppets a variety of emotions, and attempt in this way to capture the interest of the audience." That Chikamatsu had mastered the requirements of the puppet theatre was demonstrated by the series of plays he wrote between 1705 and 1725, the most brilliant period in the history of the *jōruri*.

There must have been in Chikamatsu's day critics who believed that realism was the one thing most to be sought by dramatists and producers. Chikamatsu understood that realism ran counter to the art of the puppet theatre and the *kabuki* as well, as the following account of one of his conversations demonstrates.

" Someone said, ' People nowadays will not accept plays unless they are realistic and well reasoned out. There are many things in the old stories which people will not now tolerate. It is thus that such people as *kabuki* actors are considered skilful to the degree that their acting resembles reality. The first consideration is to have the retainer in the play resemble a real retainer, and to have the daimyō look like a real daimyō. People will not stand for the childish nonsense they did in the past.' Chikamatsu answered, ' Your view seems like a plausible one, but it is a theory which does not take into account the real methods of art. Art is something which lies in the slender margin between the real and the unreal. Of course it seems desirable, in view of the current taste for realism, to have the retainer in the play copy the gestures and speech of a real retainer, but in that case should a real retainer of a daimyō put rouge and powder on his face like an actor ? Or, would it prove entertaining if an actor, on the grounds that real retainers do not make up their faces, were to appear on the stage and perform, with his beard growing wild and his head shaven ? This is what I mean by the slender margin between the real and the unreal. It is unreal, and yet it is not unreal ; it is real, and yet it is not real. Entertainment lies between the two.

" ' In this connection, there is the story of a certain court lady who had a lover. The two loved each other very passionately, but the lady lived far deep in the women's palace, and the man could not visit her quarters. She could see him therefore only very rarely, from between the cracks of her screen of state at the court. She longed for him so desperately that she had a wooden image carved of the man. Its appearance was not like that of any ordinary doll, but did not differ in any particle from the man. It goes without saying that the colour of his complexion was perfectly rendered ; even the pores of his skin were delineated. The openings in his ears and nostrils were fashioned, and there was no discrepancy even in the number of teeth in the mouth. Since it was made with the man posing beside it, the only difference between the man and this doll was the presence in one, and the absence in the other, of a soul. However, when the lady drew the doll close to her and looked at it, the exactness of the reproduction of the living man chilled her, and she felt unpleasant and rather frightened. Court lady that she was, her love was also chilled, and as she found it distressing to have the doll by her side, she soon threw it away.

" ' In view of this we can see that if one makes an exact copy of a living being, even if it happened to be Yang Kuei-fei, one will become disgusted with it. Thus, if when one paints an image or carves it of wood there are, in the name of artistic licence, some stylized parts in a work otherwise resembling the real form ; this is, after all, what people love in art. The same is true of literary composition. While bearing resemblance to the original, it should have stylization ; this makes it art, and is what delights men's minds. . . .' [1]

In his puppet-plays Chikamatsu knew exactly how to keep within the slender margin between reality and unreality. In his most popular work, *The Battles of Coxinga*, there are scenes of horror which are tolerable to the audience only because of the stylization afforded by the puppets ; if it were believed for one moment that these events were actually taking place in the theatre, only a person with a very strong stomach could bear them. On the other hand, Chikamatsu could induce a suspension of disbelief with the same means, thus producing an effect of reality within basic unreality. (The suspension of disbelief is, of course, nothing new to Western audiences.) For example, in *The Battles of Coxinga* there is a fight between the hero and a tiger. Such a scene is unconvincing in print, and would be ludicrous on the stage, where the spectator would be conscious of the two men inside the tiger skin, and could not take seriously the hero's wrestlings with so ungainly a creature. Such a spectacle would be unreal without the admixture of the real that Chikamatsu insisted on. In the puppet theatre, however, the tiger is no less realistic than the hero, and there is no reason why a spectator who accepts the initial unreality of a puppet performing as a man should be unable to accept a puppet tiger as well. Thus, in the same play the puppets could bring unreality to a scene which would otherwise be too painful to watch, or reality to a scene which would otherwise merely be comical. In neither case is the effect achieved either reality or

[1] Quoted in Keene, pp. 95–6.

unreality, but that in-between state that Chikamatsu sought or that Yeats meant when he spoke of the distance that imaginative art kept from the audience.

The puppet theatre, as might be deduced from the above, is an extremely demanding medium. As long as the texts of the plays are first-rate, their value is enhanced by having them performed by puppets which are, as Claudel said, the embodiment of the words. However, the faults in any second-rate play become all too apparent under such treatment. It is like having a company of actors whose exclusive concern is to pronounce the lines of a play perfectly, without any attempt at interpretation or characterization, thus suppressing their own personalities for the sake of the texts. If the plays thus being performed are by Shakespeare, they may well gain a great deal, but most plays will not stand up to such treatment. This is always true of the puppet theatre, for none of the charm or individual talent of the accomplished actor can save the faulty text.

The texts of Chikamatsu's plays, masterpieces though some of them are, do not always read very well because they were designed with the special requirements of the puppet stage in mind. In contrast with the muted world of the *Nō* drama, we find elaborately framed speeches and descriptive passages, well suited to puppet performance. However, Chikamatsu wrote not only heroic plays like *The Battles of Coxinga*, but also domestic tragedies based on incidents of contemporary life. The principal characters of these plays are from the middle and lower classes—merchants, clerks, bandits, prostitutes. Although these are unmistakably puppet-plays, the subjects and the texts lend themselves far more readily to adaptation by actors than those of the heroic plays, as may easily be imagined. A battle between a man and a tiger can scarcely be made credible on a normal stage, but the tragic story of the love of a debt-ridden tradesman for a prostitute, when performed by actors, can acquire additional pathos by reducing the distance between the audience and the character. The danger here is that the appetite for realism will be whetted by this first concession, and that the poetic dialogue will be replaced by more " natural " prose, that the conventional dramatic usages such as the journey of the two lovers will be suppressed ; in short, that the play as conceived by Chikamatsu will disappear in favour of a work possessing the kind of realism he so deplored.

In Chikamatsu's own day, the most popular of his works by far was *The Battles of Coxinga*, one of his most imaginative creations. It is estimated that it was seen by 240,000 people at one theatre alone during the 17 months of its initial run— this in a city whose population did not exceed 300,000. The play was imitated by various other writers, and in due course it was adapted for use by actors. But it was from about this time that the actors began to imitate the movements of the puppets, thus attempting to preserve some of the stylization. Yeats was fascinated when he saw a Japanese actor perform in this manner, and noted in the stage direction to his own play *At the Hawk's Well* that all the persons of the work should suggest marionettes in their movements.

The puppets eventually lost in popularity to the actors in Japan, although the art continues to be practised on a small scale, chiefly, like the *Nō*, for the enjoyment of connoisseurs. Comparing the two, the *Nō* is clearly more poetic, and altogether couched on a higher aesthetic plane than the *jōruri*. It is noble and remote—one might almost say Aeschylean. Or, to give an analogy drawn from Western music, the *Nō* is like the operas of Monteverdi or Handel—beautiful and expressive, but not particularly dramatic. The slow miming and dancing which usually so weary the foreign visitor to a *Nō* performance have the same function as one of Handel's long arias ; not to advance the action of the play, but to communicate to us something more than words alone can express about the character who is singing or dancing. With the *jōruri* we move to a world like that of the operas of Gluck or Mozart. It is interesting, in this connection, that some of Mozart's earlier operas have successfully been performed with marionettes, and critics often say of *Cosi Fan Tutti*, that it seems to have been written for them. In these operas, as in the *jōruri*, there is a greater fusion of the words and the music, a more obvious attempt to interest the audience in what will happen next. But there is still a stylization and a nobility which vanish in later operatic developments, just as these qualities in *jōruri* tended to disappear in the *kabuki*. Thus, Eurydice, insisting that Orpheus turn around to look at her, remains distant and beautiful, while Fricka arguing with Wotan in Valhalla is somehow commonplace.

We need not push this parallel any further—it is not an exact one in any case. Although the *Nō* and the *jōruri* plays can be appreciated fully only in performance, they are not merely the libretti of essentially musical productions. They are works of poetic drama, and at a time when our playwrights seem increasingly to be turning to this medium, they may well find help if not inspiration in the achievements of the Japanese theatre.

IV. THE JAPANESE NOVEL

THE novel has a longer history in Japan than in any other country, and has sometimes attained heights rarely reached elsewhere. It is difficult to say just when the first Japanese novel was written, if only because the definition of the word " novel " itself is so uncertain. If we adopt some arbitrary definition, such as calling any work of fiction in prose over 100 pages in length a novel, we may then say that there are Japanese novels as far back as the tenth century, and that the tradition has remained unbroken to this day.

The Japanese novel had a double origin. There were first of all the anecdotes and tales such as are found in the earliest books. Many of these may have been passed down from generation to generation as part of the national folklore, but there were also stories of Chinese and Indian origin, which came in with the introduction of Buddhism. Such stories ranged in length from a few lines to a dozen or more pages, and, although their contents were highly varied, tales of the strange and miraculous predominated, as one might expect in view of the religious inspiration of most of them.

These stories, often of a fantastic nature, furnished part of the background for the novel. The other important source lay in Japanese poetry. I have mentioned the obscurity of much Japanese verse. The shortness of the commonly used forms was such that, in the attempt to impart as much suggestive power as possible, the poets often left out such obvious information as might be necessary for the comprehension of their verses. This may have been the reason why so many of the early poems have short prose prefaces describing the circumstances under which they were composed. Thus, if the preface says that the verse was presented to a friend about to depart on a sea-journey, the words " you may be tossed about " presumably refer to the motion of the boat, rather than to any other possibility which the unelucidated words might possess. Sometimes the prefaces were longer than the poems they introduce ; we can see how it might happen that a poet, instead of confining himself to the bare mention of his wife's death, or whatever else had occasioned a poem, would tell in the preface about the love which the two had shared. The verse that followed then might be on the brevity of life, or any other suitable topic, the interest of the verse being increased by our knowledge of the particular circumstances under which it was written. In a similar manner, we can imagine how in later times someone, finding the poems left by a famous writer, might attempt in editing them to give the backgrounds of these poems, either from stories he had heard about the poet, or from his own intuitions. This may have been the origin of *The Tales of Ise*, a tenth-century work often attributed to Ariwara no Narihira. In this book we have 125 episodes, each built around one or more poems. There is no unified conception behind these little stories, although if we assume that the unnamed man who is the hero of most of them was Narihira himself, we may be able to consider *The Tales of Ise* as a kind of *Vita Nuova*, with the prose parts serving as explanations for the poems. But the organization of the book is so loose, and the connections between the episodes so tenuous, that no single narrative can be evolved, even of the kind which Shakespeare's *Sonnets* have sometimes inspired.

The subject-matter of the poem-tales (if so we may style works in the genre of *The Tales of Ise*) was drawn, unlike the fantastic tales, from ordinary life. Many of the episodes concern some nobleman who, while hunting in a distant part of the country, falls in love with a village girl. The style and the manner of incorporating the poems into the episodes is most easily revealed by a section from *The Tales of Ise* such as the following one :

"There once lived a man in a remote village. One day, announcing to his beloved that he was going to the court for service there, he took a fond leave of her and departed. For three years he did not return, and the lady, having in loneliness waited so long for him, finally consented to spend the night with another man, who had been very kind to her. That very night her old lover returned. When he knocked at the door, asking her to unbolt it, she answered him through the door with this poem. 'For three years I waited in loneliness, and just this night someone else is sharing my pillow.' He replied, 'Try then to love him as much as I have loved you through all these years.' With this poem he started away, but the lady called out, 'Whatever has happened or not happened, my heart is still, as it was before, yours.' But the man did not turn back. Stricken with grief, she followed after him, but could not manage to catch up. In a place where a clear stream flowed, she fell, and there with blood from her finger she wrote on a stone, 'I could not detain him—he went without a thought for me, and now shall I vanish.' Thus she wrote, and there she died."

If one reads just the four poems contained in this episode, one sees that they narrate the entire story, although not so clearly as when supplemented by the prose description. It may have been originally by way of a commentary on the poems that the tales were composed.

One of the early novels which most clearly shows the two

sources, the strange story and the poem-tale, is *The Hollow Tree,* a work of the tenth century. In the first part of the book is related the story of a musician who journeys to distant countries, as far even as Persia, in search of some magic wood with which to make lutes. After many curious adventures, the man finds the wood, but it is guarded by monsters. Only with the aid of supernatural intervention is he able to carry any wood back to Japan to make his wonderful musical instruments. The rest of this part of *The Hollow Tree* is conceived in the fantastic vein of the earlier short-stories. But in the second part of the novel, concerned mainly with an account of the Princess Atemiya and her suitors, we are taken into a far more realistic world, and the influence of the poem-tale is conspicuous. *The Hollow Tree* contains some 986 poems, which is almost as high a proportion as *The Tales of Ise.* It is a curious book in every way, representing an undigested set of influences. But as it moves towards its close *The Hollow Tree* acquires considerable power, as if the author were gradually gaining confidence in the new literary medium. It is, in a sense, a history of the development of the early Japanese novel. It has every feature of a missing link save that it is not missing. It affords us exactly the kind of transition which we might have conjectured between *The Tales of Ise* and *The Tale of Genji,* written about 1000 A.D.

When the first volume of Arthur Waley's translation of *The Tale of Genji* appeared in 1923, Western critics, astonished at its grandeur and at the unsuspected world which it revealed to them, searched desperately for parallels in more familiar literature. *The Tale of Genji* was likened to *Don Quixote, The Decameron, Gargantua and Pantagruel, Tom Jones,* even to *Le Morte d'Arthur* ; in short, to almost every major work of fiction with such notable exceptions as *Moby Dick.* The relative suitability of such parallels will be clear after a brief consideration of the nature of the book, and of its author, Lady Murasaki.

The Tale of Genji would seem to be a conspicuous exception to many of the generalizations I have made about the qualities of Japanese literature. Far from being a work of cryptic brevity, it runs to some 2,500 pages in most editions. Older novels, such as The Hollow Tree, were quite long too, but the faultiness of their construction generally resulted in the books falling into clearly defined and almost independent segments. The Tale of Genji is not constructed in accordance with any Western novelist's conception, but possesses rather the form of one of the horizontal scrolls for which Japan is famous. They often start with just a few figures, gradually develop into scenes of great complexity and excitement, and as gradually dwindle back into a cluster of men, then a horse, then, almost lost in the mist, a last solitary soldier. In its magnitude and its sureness of technique, The Tale of Genji is indeed exceptional, yet the work is clearly the product of purely Japanese traditions. It represents the culmination of all that had gone before, and at the same time its central importance makes it the most typical as well as the greatest work of Japanese literature. It was a classic in its own day and, devotedly read and annotated by emperors and philosophers, as well as by all manner of ordinary people, it has inspired a great deal of other literature and art. When in the seventeenth century an era of peace and prosperity followed centuries of terrible wars, it was to The Tale of Genji that the wealthy merchants turned for the model of the life they wished to enjoy, and novelists forgot six centuries of gloom in re-creating Genjis of their own. That the influence of The Tale of Genji still survives, is evidenced by its great importance in the work of Tanizaki, perhaps the leading Japanese novelist of our day. Now, thanks to Arthur Waley's superb translation, it is available to Western readers, who can now judge for themselves whether it is not only the world's first real novel, but one of its greatest.

About the author of *The Tale of Genji*, Lady Murasaki (*c.* 975–*c.* 1025), we know few facts, but we fortunately still have her diary, which affords us interesting insights into her character. She says of herself :

> " That I am very vain, reserved, unsociable, wanting always to keep people at a distance—that I am wrapped up in the study of ancient stories, conceited, living all the time in a poetical world of my own and scarcely realizing the existence of other people, save occasionally to make spiteful and depreciatory comments upon them—such is the opinion of me that most strangers hold, and they are prepared to dislike me accordingly.   But when they get to know me, they find to their extreme surprise that I am kind and gentle—in fact, quite a different person from the monster they had imagined ; as indeed many have afterwards confessed.   Nevertheless, I know that I have been definitely set down at Court as an ill-natured censorious prig.   Not that I mind very much, for I am used to it and see that it is due to things in my nature which I cannot possibly change.   The Empress has often told me that, though I seemed always bent upon not giving myself away in the royal presence, yet she felt after a time as if she knew me more intimately than any of the rest." [1]

We, too, as we read *The Tale of Genji*, feel that we are learning a great deal about Lady Murasaki, especially in such asides as

> " You may think that many of the poems which I here repeat are not worthy of the talented characters to whom

[1] *The Tale of Genji*, introduction by Waley, p. xv.

attracted a man to a woman might be hearing her play a musical instrument as he passed by her quarters at night, or it might be a note in her handwriting of which he caught a glimpse, or it might be just her name. Any of these things could persuade a man that he was madly in love with a woman, and cause him to pursue her until she yielded, all this without ever having seen her except at night, or perhaps by the light of fireflies.

The only Western book of which I am reminded in reading *The Tale of Genji* is Marcel Proust's *A la Recherche du Temps Perdu*. There are striking similarities of technique between the two works, such as that of casually mentioning people or events, and only later, in a symphonic manner, developing their full meaning. But above such resemblances in manner there are the grand themes common to the two. The subject of both novels is the splendours and decline of an aristocratic society, and in both the barons are noted less for their hunting and fishing than for their surpassing musical abilities, their flawless taste and their brilliant conversation. These were snobbish societies, extremely sensitive to pedigree and rank. In *The Tale of Genji,* for instance, the young princess who is being reared as a future empress is shocked beyond words when the truth, carefully concealed from her until that moment, is disclosed that she was born in the country and not in the capital ! It is as if the Duchesse de Guermantes discovered that she had been born in some industrial suburb ! In both novels, also, there is an overpowering interest in the passage of time and its effects on society. Proust is far crueller than Lady Murasaki in describing how, with the passage of time, Mme. de Ville-parisis, for whom fortunes were once squandered by her lovers, has become a wrinkled hag, or how the odious Mme. Verdurin in time becomes Princesse de Guermantes. But if Murasaki is kinder, she is none the less insistent on the point—the dashing young men become boring and pompous state councillors, the distinguished ladies become talkative old crones. With the figures in the novel she really cares for, however, she is more merciful, killing them off before they reach an unattractive state. In contrast to Proust, who turns the glorious world he · at first pictures into a miserable company of parvenus and hideously aged aristocrats, Murasaki gradually dissolves her society into the empty spaces of her painting, leaving only a reduced figure here and there to show how great a falling-off there has been.

Murasaki gave her views on the art of the novel in a famous passage in *The Tale of Genji*. Genji, discovering one of the court-ladies deeply engrossed in reading a romance, at first teases her, then continues :

" ' As a matter of fact I think far better of this art than I have led you to suppose. Even its practical value is immense. Without it what should we know of how people lived in the past, from the Age of the Gods down to the present day ? For history-books, such as the Chronicles of Japan, show us only one small corner of life ; whereas these diaries and romances which I see piled around you contain, I am sure, the most minute information about all sorts of people's private affairs. . . .' He smiled, and went on : ' But I have a theory of my own about what this art of the novel is, and how it came into being. To begin with, it does not simply consist in the author's telling a story about the adventures of some other person. On the contrary, it happens because the storyteller's own experience of men and things, whether for good or ill—not only what he has passed through himself, but even events which he has only witnessed or been told of—has moved him to an emotion so passionate that he can no longer keep it shut up in his heart. Again and again something in his own life or in that around him will seem to the writer so important that he cannot bear to let it pass into oblivion. There must never come a time, he feels, when men do not know about it. That is my view of how this art arose.

" ' Clearly then, it is no part of the storyteller's craft to describe only what is good or beautiful. Sometimes, of course, virtue will be his theme, and he may then make such play with it as he will. But he is just as likely to have been struck by numerous examples of vice and folly in the world around him, and about them he has exactly the same feelings as about the pre-eminently good deeds which he encounters : they are important and must all be garnered in. Thus anything whatsoever may become the subject of a novel, provided only that it happens in this mundane life and not in some fairyland beyond our human ken.' " [1]

The ideas in this passage are so familiar to us because of the works of modern writers, particularly Proust, that we cannot perhaps immediately see how extraordinary they actually are. Clearly, neither the strange story nor the poem-tale, the two forerunners of the Japanese novel, attempted to give us any coherent idea of the past in a desire to preserve it from oblivion. Nor, for that matter, do we find any such intent in *The Decameron*, *Tom Jones*, nor in many other European novels before the nineteenth century. To tell a good story in such a way as to keep the reader's attention from page to page is an essential feature of every novel, but to make this story the vehicle for one's own thoughts, one's own memories and impressions, one's own feeling for the past, seems a strikingly modern method.

[1] *The Tale of Genji*, pp. 501–2.

Again, the dispassionate acceptance of all material, whether good deeds or bad ones, with no attempt at drawing a moral from them, is also an exceptionally advanced idea, especially for Japan, where it was shortly to be buried for many centuries.

It is when looking at *The Tale of Genji* in its historical surroundings that we feel most keenly its unique charm for us. We do not stand at a sufficiently great distance from the world and time of Proust to know what finally happened to the kind of people he described, but the melancholy fate of the Japanese court society is the subject of many of the novels of the twelfth to fifteenth centuries. The most famous of them, *The Tale of the Heike*, begins :

"In the sound of the bell of the Gion Temple echoes the impermanence of all things. The pale hue of the flowers of the teak-tree show the truth that they who prosper must fall. The proud ones do not last long, but vanish like a spring-night's dream. And the mighty ones too will perish in the end, like dust before the wind."

This is the mood of the times which succeeded Murasaki's. Less than a century after she finished *The Tale of Genji* with its picture of the most elegant society ever known, the country was torn by civil wars. The lovely capital was wasted by fires, plagues and famines. It was at one point decided to abandon the old city, and a boy emperor was taken off to a miserable mountain village. In such terrible times many men turned to religion for comfort. In *The Tale of Genji* religion plays quite an important part too, a religion which finds expression in pageantry, great ceremonies in which thousands of priests participate or in the marvellous variety of Buddhist art created for those who sought to obtain merit by rich donations to the church. The Buddhism of the centuries following Lady

Murasaki was essentially a pessimistic religion. Some sects preached the doctrine that the world had entered its last degenerate days, and that the only course left open for the religious man was to flee the world altogether and live as a hermit in the mountains. Salvation could be gained by murmuring one simple phrase rather than by costly rituals. The beautiful temples were left to rot, or were broken up for firewood by the sufferers from wars and natural disasters. At the end of the twelfth century a military dictatorship was established which, in one guise or another, lasted until 1868 and perhaps longer. For much of this long period it was the soldier, and not the aristocrat, who figured most importantly in Japanese novels. The generals whose chief occupation in *The Tale of Genji* seemed to be blending perfumes, gave way to men who slept with their swords by their pillows.

The quality of many of the novels of the period is perhaps best suggested by a fragmentary little story which, strictly speaking, does not belong to any novel at all. It is, however, typical of many of the episodes in such works as *The Tale of the Heike*. It is called *The Tale of Tokiaki*.

" When Yoshimitsu was serving as Captain of the Guards, word reached him in the capital that his elder brother, the Governor of Mutsu, had attacked the rebellious barons. He asked leave of the court to depart from the capital, and when this permission was refused, tendered his resignation as Captain of the Guards. Slinging his bowstring-bag by his side, he rode out of the capital towards the fighting.

" Just this side of Kagami, in the province of Ōmi, a man wearing a dark-blue unlined hunting-cloak and green trousers, with a strapless visor pulled down over his face, rode up behind Yoshimitsu, whipping and urging his pony forward.

Yoshimitsu was at first disturbed, but as the rider approached he could see that it was Toyohara Tokiaki. 'Why have you come here?' Yoshimitsu asked. The boy did not answer the question, but said merely, 'I am going with you.'

" Yoshimitsu attempted to dissuade him. 'It would make me very happy to have you with me, but the business which has taken me from the capital is very grave, and you would only be in the way if you came.' But the boy would not listen to him, and insisted on following. Yoshimitsu could do nothing to change his mind, and thus they travelled together as far as Ashigara Mountain in the province of Sagami. Here Yoshimitsu drew up his horse and said, ' That you have come thus far in spite of my efforts proves how strong your determination is. However, it will be an extremely difficult matter to get through the barrier at this mountain. I shall spur on my horse and break through somehow, for ever since leaving the capital I have placed no value on my life. But there is no sense in your coming any farther. Please turn back here.' But Tokiaki still would not listen to him.

" No further word was said. Yoshimitsu understood then of what Tokiaki was thinking. Leaving the road a little, they headed through the fields to some shady trees. There Yoshimitsu cut away the underbrush and dismounted. He then placed two shields on the ground, sat on one, and had Tokiaki sit on the other. Putting all worldly thoughts far from his mind, he drew from his quiver a piece of paper which he showed to Tokiaki. On it were two pieces of music in the Arabian mode written in the hand of Tokiaki's father, Tokimoto. Yoshimitsu had been a pupil of Tokimoto and had learned from him the secret of the arts of flutes and strings. Tokiaki's father having died before the boy was ten,

he had never taught him the secret.   Yoshimitsu asked, ' Do
you have your Chinese flute with you ? '   ' Yes, it is here,'
and he took it from his breast pocket.

" ' You are already very good on the easy works.   That
must be why you were so determined to follow me.'   Yoshimitsu then taught the boy the two pieces.   He said, ' My
mission is so grave a one, that I cannot tell if I shall survive.
But if, one chance in a hundred, I do return to the capital,
I hope I shall see you there.   Now, your family has furnished
the Court with musicians for many generations, and are an
essential part of it.   That is why I want you to return to the
capital and become a master of the art.'   When he had thus
spoken, the boy yielded to reason and went back."

This is the tone of the medieval novels.   It is one of loneliness, of single figures setting off for battle across landscapes
which now seem destitute of the flowering trees and all the
other charms they possessed some hundred years before.   The
music of *The Tale of Genji* was principally that of the sweet-
toned lute.   In the period of civil wars that followed, the sad
notes of a solitary flute played by a soldier on some still battle-
field sound again and again in the literature, particularly the
novels.   Many of the latter are war-tales, each with its burden
of glory and ashes.   The one with the most accounts of bitter
fighting and disasters is ironically called *The Chronicles of Great
Peace.*   In such books the narrative is occasioned chiefly by the
doings of the principal historical figures of the time, but there
are numerous digressions telling of the deaths of other brave
men, or of the fleeting moments of pleasure they enjoyed.

It would be misleading, however, to leave the impression
that the medieval period, if so we may call the eleventh to
sixteenth centuries, was a time of unrelieved gloom.   Both

the emperor's court and that of the shogun knew years of prosperity, and there continued to be a fairly considerable amount of poetry turned out at these courts which, restricted as it is to the familiar clichés, scarcely shows that changes had occurred since the glorious days when Lady Murasaki wrote. But in the characteristic literary products of the period, such as the Nō plays and the linked-verse, we find the terrible sadness and loneliness which so mark the novels. Another feature of the literature of this time was its decentralization. In earlier days almost all of the important books were written in the capital by members of the aristocracy, but with the breakdown of the central government, and the retreat to hermitages and monasteries by many sensitive people, literature came to be written in distant parts of the realm, as well as at the courts. Such literature does not have local colour in any cheerful sense of the term, but reflects the loneliness and resignation of artists cut off from the poetry-making society.

In 1600 a great battle was fought on the plains of Sekigahara, as a result of which the Tokugawa family gained supreme power in Japan. From that date until 1868, this family exercised a rule of generally benevolent but increasingly ineffectual despotism. One of the results of the peace which the Tokugawa family established, was a general economic prosperity and, towards the close of the seventeenth century, a great flaring-up of all kinds of cultural activity. In the field of the novel, the medieval tales of warfare or of the life of itinerant monks no longer suited the spirit of the times. The greatest novelist of the new age, and the first important personality in this field since the Lady Murasaki of some six centuries before, was Saikaku (1642–93). The work with which he established his reputation as a novelist—he was already well known as a *haiku* poet—was *The Man Who Spent His Life at Love-making*, a gay,

sometimes pornographic work which shows in many respects
Saikaku's indebtedness to *The Tale of Genji*. The characters
of his novels are drawn for the most part from the merchant
class, rather than from the aristocracy or the ranks of the *samurai*.
Most of his so-called novels are in reality short stories of varied
lengths based on the same general themes. Although the plots
of these tales often show great invention, Saikaku's outstanding
qualities as a novelist are his wit and style. He is often able
with a single sentence to catch a man's character or to depict
his whole way of life. For example, in describing how one
alert merchant never missed a chance to increase his fortune,
he says, " Even if he stumbled he used the opportunity to pick
up flints for lighters." Again, he says of this same man,
" Nothing delighted him more than watching over his daughter.
When the girl grew into womanhood he had a marriage-screen
made for her and, since he considered that one decorated with
views of Kyoto would make her restless to visit places she had
not yet seen, and that illustrations of *The Tale of Genji* or *The
Tales of Ise* would encourage wantonness in her mind, he had
the screen painted with busy scenes of the silver and copper
mines at Tada." These excerpts are from the *Treasury of Japan*,
a collection of stories on the theme of how to make (or lose)
a fortune. The heroes of these stories are men who permit
themselves no extravagance, realizing that the way to wealth
lies in meticulous care of the smallest details. When some
young men visit the rich merchant Fujiichi on the Seventh
Day of the New Year to seek his advice on how to become
millionaires, he at first has them kept waiting in his sitting-room.
Then :

" When the three guests had seated themselves the pounding
of an earthenware mortar could be heard from the kitchen,

and the sound fell with pleasant promise on their ears. They speculated on what was in store for them. One thought it would be miso soup and pickled whale-skin. 'No,' said the second, 'as this is our first visit of the New Year it should be miso soup and rice-cakes.' But the third, after careful reflection, settled firmly for miso soup and noodles. . . . Fujiichi then came into the room and talked to the three of them on the requisites for a successful career. Then he concluded, 'You have been talking with me since early in the evening, and you may think it high time the supper was served. But one way to become a millionaire is not to provide supper. The noise of the mortar which you heard when you first arrived was the pounding of starch for the paper covers of the great ledger.' " [1]

Not all of Saikaku's stories are as humorous as this one, but even in his accounts of women who go mad for love, or of young men put to death for crimes of which they were innocent, the author maintains a detachment from the story which may remind us of Fielding in *Tom Jones*. At every point he contrives to show the comic features of an apparently serious tale. His books and those of other novelists of the time are sometimes called *ukiyo* literature. *Ukiyo* is a term which formerly had been used in the sense of the " sad world ", but, by taking another meaning of the word *uki*, *ukiyo* came at this time to mean " the floating world ". This was the perfect description of the new society. Change, which had formerly been considered a sad phenomenon, as expressed in the falling of the cherry-blossoms or the scattering of the autumn leaves, now came to stand for all that was most desirable. Everyone wanted to be up to date, and novelty was the goal not only of the

[1] From an unpublished translation by G. W. Sargent.

writers of popular fiction, but of such eminently respectable
people as the poet Bashō. A frequent motif in the art of the
time is that of waves, the most dramatically changing of forms.
The fleeting pleasures of life were more prized than the eternal
values which the medieval recluses had sought. In their desire
to recapture the pleasures of the day, the writers and artists
sometimes went far beyond the bounds of decency, and from
time to time the government adopted measures against pornographic works. But in a society where the licensed quarters
were the centre of artistic life, and their denizens the subjects
of most novels, plays and prints, it was perhaps too much to
demand any reticence in calling a spade a spade.

The humour in the novels of the late seventeenth and eighteenth centuries is apt to be topical, and much has therefore
perished, leaving us with little more than an impression of the
vitality and zest for living of the authors. So much cannot be
said of the writings of Bakin (1767–1848), the last major novelist
before the Meiji Restoration of 1868. Bakin, in reaction to
the immorality of the novels of his immediate predecessors,
declared that the purpose of his books was to " encourage
virtue and reprimand vice ". This he did in an immense bulk
of writing, much of which is quite unreadable today. Bakin
not only wrote original novels, but also adapted some of the
more famous Chinese works in this form. Up to his time,
the influence of the Chinese novel had been very slight in
Japan, which was a most fortunate thing. Although Chinese
influence was the essential factor in the development of many
aspects of Japanese culture, in literature it often proved harmful,
unless thoroughly digested. Anything written in Japan in
direct imitation of Chinese models, however highly valued it
may have been in its day, is now completely dead. Those
contemporaries of Lady Murasaki who prided themselves on

their poems and essays in Chinese are now quite forgotten, and the least interesting poem in any of the famous anthologies of Japanese verse has probably been read more often than the best poem in the Chinese manner. Bakin's novels, to the degree that they are derivative from Chinese precedents, are already falling into oblivion, even though fifty years ago he was considered by most Japanese to be the greatest of their novelists.

It is hard to give any idea with mere extracts of what Bakin is like, because the whole effect of his artistic method was achieved by drowning the inadequacies in the plot with a flood of beautiful words. The closest approximation to his style is perhaps obtained in the highly inaccurate Victorian translation of the novel entitled *The Moon Shining Through a Cloud-Rift on a Rainy Night*. The boy Tajikichi has just shot a hawk, and now rather regrets killing the bird. His sister speaks first.

" ' Ah ! ' sadly ejaculated Taye ; then, noticing the scroll, added, ' What is that tied to its leg ? '

" Her brother cut the silk cord, and, seeing the seal, exclaimed—

" ' This is a letter from our honourable father ! I have killed his loyal messenger ! ' As he spoke, he reverently pressed the scroll to his forehead, then, removing the fastening, read a few words ; when big tears dropped from his red eyelids, and his bosom heaved with grief. After a moment he controlled his emotion, and said—' Honourable elder sister, this is from our honourable father—written when he was about to start upon the lonely road.' " [1]

This is bad enough to be at once a parody of Bakin and of translation from the Chinese in general. Although the language

[1] Translated by Edward Greey, p. 205.

of the original is Japanese, even metrical Japanese, the sentiments are Chinese. Or, rather, we may say that they are a Japanese piece of chinoiserie, bearing the same relation to the originals as our eighteenth-century porcelains and furniture to the real Chinese style.

It must be admitted that the Japanese novel in the early nineteenth century had dropped to its lowest level, tending to be either collections of jokes in doubtful taste, or else dreary moralizing tales in many volumes. It was a denatured literature, possessing little of the elegance of style or evocative power of the famous novels of earlier days. The 250 years of peace had created interesting new problems which should have been the subjects of novels, but the censorship made it impossible for writers to undertake them. The peasant revolts, corrupt governments, awakening interest in Europe, which mark early nineteenth-century Japan, could not be discussed by novelists. Certain contemporary events of a politically inoffensive character might be treated with impunity if suitably disguised, but nothing bordering on the nature of dangerous thoughts could be treated. The writers were thus forced to restrict themselves to hackneyed subjects which could not have engrossed them very deeply, or to trivialities of a most perishable nature.

It was the impact of the West which was to bring new life to Japanese literature, and we have not yet seen the full effects of this, even in our own day.

V. JAPANESE LITERATURE UNDER WESTERN INFLUENCE

THE first Europeans to visit Japan were some Portuguese adventurers who reached one of the outlying islands in 1542. Seven years later St. Francis Xavier introduced Christianity to the country with considerable success, and for almost a hundred years from the time of the first Portuguese visitors, the Japanese engaged in trade and other relations with Europeans, including Portuguese, Spaniards, Dutch and English. Converts to Christianity were made even among important members of the military aristocracy, and some Japanese dignitaries went on embassies to Europe and America, chiefly in connection with religious matters. But increasingly repressive measures against Christianity were adopted by the government, beginning in the late sixteenth century, in an effort to wipe out what was considered to be a threat to the security of the country. The government feared that Christian converts might divide political loyalties, and might even facilitate the invasion of the country by a European power. The example of the Philippines, conquered by the Spaniards in the sixteenth century after intense missionary activity, served as a warning to the Japanese, and by 1639 both the Spaniards and Portuguese had been forbidden to visit the country. Of the other nations which had traded with Japan, England had left voluntarily, finding the business unprofitable. The Dutch remained and were the only Europeans allowed in Japan until the country was opened to foreigners in the middle of the nineteenth century.

During the time that the Catholic missionaries were most active in Japan, at the end of the sixteenth century, they printed a number of books there, both to teach religion to their converts and for their own use as manuals of instruction in the Japanese language. The only important European literary work of a non-religious character which was translated into Japanese at this time was *Aesop's Fables*, although some scholars believe that at least the general outlines of the story of the *Odyssey* were transmitted to their Japanese acquaintances by the foreigners. This, they say, is evidenced by the curious set of stories dating from the seventeenth century about a man named Yuriwaka, whose name itself they derive in part from that of Ulysses. These stories tell of the adventures of a man who, after scoring a great triumph abroad, is abandoned on the way back to Japan at a lonely island by his wicked companions. With much difficulty the man Yuriwaka returns to his country, to find his wife the subject of the unwanted attention of various suitors. He arrives just at the time of the New Year festivities, and as part of the amusements of the day several men attempt to bend the iron bow that Yuriwaka left behind, but all fail. Whereupon Yuriwaka takes up the bow and bends it to good effect, shooting the most troublesome of his wife's suitors. He is thereupon recognized by members of the court, reunited to his wife and granted high rank.

The resemblances in the story to the *Odyssey* are evident, and some of the other episodes show similarity to parts of Camoens' epic *The Lusiads*. However, certain Japanese scholars have adduced arguments to show that the elements in the story are indigenous, and that resemblances to European works are mere coincidence. If the story of Yuriwaka was indeed a case of European influence on Japanese literature, it was the first, and remained the only important one for 150 years, for with the prohibition of Christianity and the virtual annihilation of the converts in 1637–8, Japanese lost all contact with European literature.

From time to time in the seventeenth and early eighteenth centuries European works of an obviously practical nature, such as texts of astronomy or botany, were admitted to the country, either in the original languages, or in Chinese translations made by the Jesuits in Peking. But it was not until the close of the eighteenth century that any interest was shown in European writings of a more literary nature. It was at this time that the Japanese first began to concern themselves with what they might learn from the few Dutch traders who were kept virtual prisoners on an island off Nagasaki, and a number of scholars went there to find out what they could about the West. One of them heard this story :

" Some ten years ago a ship was stranded on an island, and two men of the crew went ashore to look for water. There they encountered a giant over ten feet tall with one eye in the middle of his forehead. The giant was pleased to find the two men. He seized them and took them off with him to a rocky cavern. Inside there was another giant, the mate of the first one. The cave was spacious, with cracks in the rocks serving as windows. There were many beasts inside.

" One of the giants went out and the opening was shut as before. The other giant caught the two men and stared at them for a long time. Suddenly he seized one of them and began to eat him from the head downwards. The other man looked on in terror and astonishment as though he were watching demons in a nightmare. He could not think how he might escape. While the giant was devouring half of the first man, the other covered his face and could not bear to look. The giant then fell into a drunken sleep, snoring like thunder.

" The man pondered how he might safely escape. Finally he made up his mind and gouged out the giant's eye with his dagger. The giant let out a great cry and ran wildly about in his rage. He groped around for the man, who was, however, lying flat on the floor of the cave. The giant, for all his ferocity, could not find the man because of his blindness. Then he opened the entrance to the cave a little and drove out the animals. One by one he let them out, apparently resolved thus to catch and kill the man. The man was trapped, but he quickly caught hold under the belly of a huge boar. The giant let the animal out, not realizing the trick that had been played on him. The man was thus able to escape to his ship, which at once set sail." [1]

It is interesting to speculate how this bit of the *Odyssey* happened to reach the ears of a traveller to Nagasaki in 1774. Perhaps it was a final remnant of the material which had been used for the Yuriwaka stories, or perhaps it came more directly from one of the Dutch traders. It was in any case the type of European literature most likely to interest the Japanese ; one of the first translations of a work of European belles-lettres was the *Record of Wanderings* " written by an Englishman, Robinson Crusoe ".

For the most part, however, the enthusiasts for European learning in the late eighteenth and early nineteenth centuries confined themselves to books of science and general information, if only because a Dutch novel or play would have been far too difficult for any but the most skilful interpreters, while a Dutch mathematical book could be deciphered by anyone familiar with the general principles of that science.

From about 1860 there were Japanese translations of European

[1] Translated in Keene, *The Japanese Discovery of Europe*, pp. 95–6.

novels and poetry, often crude, but very popular. Most of the
translations were from English, the language preferred by
Japanese once they had discovered that the Dutch which they
had so painfully mastered in the days before the opening of
the ports was of little use in dealing with English and American
traders. The choice of books for translation was dictated in
part by the necessity of finding works which were readily
intelligible to Japanese readers. Thus, a novel by Jules Verne,
for all its fantasy, was not difficult for Japanese to understand,
for it required only the confidence in the progress of science
which they quickly acquired. On the other hand, a novel by
Dickens such as *Bleak House* would have been virtually un-
intelligible because the complex society which it described
could not be demonstrated to Japanese readers like the workings
of a locomotive, nor did it represent a European version of
problems with which they were familiar at home.

The first important monument in the creation of a new
Japanese literature in which the lessons from the West were
incorporated came with *The Essence of the Novel* written by
Tsubouchi Shōyō (1859–1935), published in 1885. Tsubouchi,
deploring the poor quality of the literature of his time, sought
to analyse what was wrong with it, and how it might be
rectified. For the first time, he said, improved methods of
printing had made it possible for there to be an almost un-
limited circulation of books, and this had initially resulted in
the publication of huge numbers of clumsy imitations of Bakin
and other early nineteenth-century writers, for want of any
new ideas. Such works conformed on the surface to the
doctrine that literature is for the encouragement of virtue, and
contained various pseudo-moral elements, but they were in
reality of an extremely low order. Whose fault was this,
asked Tsubouchi, and answered that it resulted not only from

the inferiority of the writers but also from the lack of discrimination on the part of readers. He wrote, "It has long been the custom in our country to consider the novel as a device for education, and its chief function is frequently proclaimed to be the encouragement or chastisement of morals, but in practice the only books which are read are horror stories or works of pornography." According to Tsubouchi the way out of the literary difficulties in which Japan found herself was to adopt the Western view of literature and abandon the old concept of literature as an instrument of didactic intent. He had heard an American scholar speak in Tokyo about the meaning of art, and subscribed to his views. According to him, art fulfilled its functions to the extent that it was completely decorative, for was not something which entertained people and elevated their tastes an essential thing to society?

Tsubouchi's arguments approach the familiar belief in art for art's sake, but he was not content with merely urging Japanese to abandon their old views on the function of literature ; he called for new forms which were better suited to the complexity of modern man than verses in 31 syllables or tales of wild adventure. He declared, " How extremely uncomplex a thing Japanese verse of all sorts appears when compared with Western poetry . . . When I say this I may be slandering the poetry of the Imperial Land as being very crude, but with the general development of culture and the advance of our knowledge by several stages, our emotions cannot help changing and becoming more complex. The men of old were simple and they had straightforward emotions. Thus they could vent their full feelings with just 31 syllables, but we cannot completely express all we feel with so few words."

Tsubouchi's remarks have been quoted at some length because of their great historical significance. He was one of the first

Japanese to have had a good understanding of European literature, and, incidentally, made a complete translation of Shakespeare's works which remains the standard one in Japan. He
was perhaps the key figure in the development of literary taste
in the country, attempting as he did to create a Japanese literature
which would bear comparison with that produced in England
and in other parts of Europe. He sought to find examples in
the earlier Japanese literature of parallels to the things which
he praised in European literature, and so to give a native tradition
for writers to follow. Thus, he rejected the plays of Chikamatsu
which had fantastic elements, in favour of the domestic tragedies
which could more easily be compared with European plays.
Realism and complexity were the two things he advocated in
all forms of literature.

The great problem for Japanese who sought to write in the
new style was also touched on by Tsubouchi. Western literature
in the late nineteenth century was dominated by the expression
of individual impressions and beliefs. A century before, Rous-
seau had begun his confessions with the assertion that regardless
of whether he was better or worse than other men he was
certainly different, and this attitude coloured the entire romantic
movement. In Japan there existed no such tradition of in-
dividualism, at least not since the civil wars of the twelfth
century and afterwards had led to the formation of a rigid
feudal society, where the claims of the individual were sternly
denied. When we read Lady Murasaki's diary, written in the
early eleventh century, we feel that she is a complex living
being, whom we can understand, but even the most personal
writings of the eight centuries that followed her time seldom
arouse any such feeling. One has the impression always that
people are acting within a situation which has implicit in it
certain regular reactions. At first these reactions have to be

learned as a part of everyday etiquette, but later they become
the spontaneous expression of feelings. Thus, in taking leave
of one's host after a party one had to apologize for one's bad
behaviour, and thus when viewing the falling cherry-blossoms
or foam on the water, one had to utter exclamations on the
brevity of life. A pattern of behaviour was developed which
all but cancelled out individual preferences. This gives a certain
ornamental flatness to the people of history and fiction. We
are perhaps most aware of this quality in the plays, where
there is no real attempt at characterization. There is nothing
in the personalities of the heroes of Chikamatsu's plays to distinguish them one from the other. Given the different set of
circumstances, they would behave in exactly the same manner
as their counterparts in other plays. In poetry too the prevail-
ing note is one of impersonality, rather than that of the romantic
cry from the poet's heart. The reluctance to use the word
" I " may remind us of our own Augustan poets, but the subjects of the poetry, unlike the general truths of the *Essay on
Man*, are brief flashes of perception and would seem to us to
require a greater personal touch. In the long centuries between
Lady Murasaki's day and the late nineteenth century, there is
seldom a voice that speaks to us with a truly personal note.

The blame for this situation may be laid on the feudal society
and its dictates, but it should not be imagined, however, that
Japanese writers were impatiently waiting for a liberation so
that they might express their pent-up individual sentiments.
As Tsubouchi indicated, complex emotional reactions could be
developed only along with other Western accomplishments.
And though it was relatively easy for poets to write stanzas
of irregular lengths instead of the *tanka* or for novelists to turn
from the style of their predecessors in favour of works closely
approaching European realism, the expression or creation of

individuality remained, and I think still remains, the great problem. Again and again the European reader is likely to ask of a character in a novel or a play, " What is he *really* thinking ? " Only gradually does one come to the conclusion that he is really thinking just what he says, or if he is silent, just what the conventional response would be. This tends in a way to make modern Japanese writing harder for us to understand than the older varieties. That is, when we read a book describing the court life of the eleventh century, we enter a completely unfamiliar world and are prepared to accept all its curiosities. Did the ladies in *The Tale of Genji* blacken their teeth to attain greater elegance ? Very well, we say, they did. But when we read a novel in which the characters worry about vitamin shortages, spend their Sunday afternoons taking photos with a miniature camera, and model their coiffure on that of their favourite Hollywood star, we do not expect to find emotional blanks behind the characters, and when we do it is most disconcerting. Thus, in Tanizaki's novel *The Thin Snow* (1946–9), where the central theme is the finding of a husband for a young lady, we are at no point told what her reactions are to the search, what she thinks of her different suitors, or even of the man she is finally to marry. We expect at least to find hints of Freudian repression or some other literary device which belongs to the same world as vitamin shortages. The submissive and inarticulate Japanese lady seems altogether remote.

If Tsubouchi's *Essence of the Novel* did not lead to any general outburst of individual emotions, it did encourage the development of types of fiction previously unknown in Japan. European realism, as found in the numerous translations of mid-Victorian novelists and, to a lesser extent, certain Russian writers, led Japanese to turn from the ponderous historical romances or the fantastic stories which Tsubouchi so deplored to accounts of contemporary life. The first important novel to follow Tsubouchi's essay was *The Drifting Cloud* (1887–9) by Futabatei Shimei (1864–1909), a work which is often considered the pioneer novel of the new literary movement. This is the story of a young man, a member of the emancipated intelligentsia, who leaves his job in the Civil Service to live in the country in his uncle's house. He is ineffectual and irresolute, earning the scorn of his aunt, a woman of peasant disposition, and eventually of his cousin, with whom he is in love. The cousin finally marries another man, but the unhappy hero is still unable to arouse enough energy to do anything. *The Drifting Cloud* can scarcely be said to boast a plot, but when compared with the other novels which were being written in its day, its importance can quickly be realized. Here was a leading character who, far from possessing the ability to quell demons, like the heroes of most of Bakin's novels, is thoroughly mediocre in every way. Sometimes he arouses our pity, but seldom our real sympathy. Foreign influence, particularly the writings of Turgenev, was important in Futabatei's work. This he shows not only in his manner of telling the story, but in the language he uses. Novels written in Japan during previous centuries were couched for the most part in the literary language, an artificial, sometimes highly ornamented style. Futabatei's readings in Turgenev and other European writers convinced him that the language of books must be the same as that which is used in speech. *The Drifting Cloud* is the first novel to have been written under this principle, and it was of great importance, both in its subject-matter and style. With few exceptions all subsequent novelists abandoned both the traditional types of subject and the traditionally employed language.

The quantity of literature produced during the Meiji era

(1868–1912) was vast. Much of it is no longer of any real interest, but this is not surprising, for neither is much of the literature produced in England during the same period. Some of it, particularly the novels and poetry written in the first flush of enthusiasm for Western ways, is distinctly comic today, as for example this poem translated by Sansom :

O Liberty, Ah Liberty, Liberty O !
Liberty, we two are plighted until the world ends.
And who shall part us ? Yet in this world there are
clouds that hide the moon and winds that destroy the
blossoms. Man is not master of his fate.
      It is a long tale to tell
      But once upon a time
      There were men who wished
      To give the people Liberty
      And set up a republican government.
      To that end. . . .[1]

But it is really unfair to deride such poems or the translation of *The Bride of Lammermoor* entitled " A Spring Breeze Love Story ". They were products of the dilemma of Japanese writers faced at the same time with an avalanche of new ideas and new ways of expressing them, and with the problem of how much, if anything, to retain of the old ideas and ways. The man who wrote the ode to liberty, with its utterly foreign ideas, nevertheless used the Japanese images of the clouds that hide the moon and the winds that destroy the blossoms. Similarly, even in novels written after *The Drifting Cloud* there were usually passages or themes or solutions which seem false to the new medium, although they are true to Japan.

The conflict between old and new forms of expression is

[1] Sansom, *The Western World and Japan*, p. 428.

apparent in the writings of Natsume Sōseki (1867–1916), often considered as the most important novelist of the period. His works are *tranches de la vie* in the naturalistic manner of late nineteenth-century European literature, by which he was much influenced. However, Natsume's naturalism did not lead him to the portrayal of the lower depths of society, as frequently in European works. He preferred instead to treat the day-to-day experiences of quite ordinary people, usually of the middle class. Sometimes Natsume describes moments when the lives of such people are touched by dramatic events, but he was especially interested in the quiet routine of daily living. Natsume's works still delight Japanese, largely because of his beautiful style, but a Western reader may find the oriental calm achieved by Natsume to be at times insufficiently engrossing.

The novel of the Meiji era which I believe has the greatest interest for the Western reader of today is *The Broken Commandment* (1906) by Shimazaki Tōson (1872–1943). This is the story of a young man who is a member of the *eta* or pariah class.[1] Although discrimination against members of this class has long been prohibited by law, feeling is still rather strong among Japanese on the subject, and fifty years ago it must have been far more intense. The young man of the novel is commanded by his father never under any circumstances to reveal to others that he is an *eta*, and he manages in fact to conceal it from even his closest friends during the time that he is at school, and later, when he becomes a teacher. But he cannot help showing his sympathy for the *eta* in spite of all his efforts to keep the vow

[1] The *eta* are an outcast class in Japan, somewhat resembling the untouchables of India. Their traditional occupations included those of butcher, tanner, sandal-maker, etc. Although it has been forbidden since 1871 to discriminate against *eta*, or even to refer to them by that name, the prejudice against them still persists.

he made to his father. When an *eta* is thrown out of the inn
where Ushimatsu, the hero, lodges, he immediately moves,
even though he knows that this action may arouse suspicion.
Again, when an *eta* boy at the school can find no one else with
whom to play tennis, Ushimatsu joins with him. But it is
especially in the interest he shows towards the writings of an
eta who has become a celebrated champion of the class that
Ushimatsu, in his own eyes at least, reveals his identity. He
accordingly in a moment of fright sells all the books he has
by the *eta* author and denies to others that he has any special
interest in him. Later, when this author visits the town,
Ushimatsu sees him secretly. He longs to tell him that he
too is an *eta*, but, remembering his father's commandment,
controls himself. It becomes increasingly difficult for him to
hide his anxiety and depression from his friends, who almost
push him to the point of revealing his secret. Then, quite by
chance, the director of the school, who is unfriendly to Ushimatsu, learns that the young man is an *eta*. The fact spreads
among the teachers of the school, and finally to the pupils just
at the moment when Ushimatsu decides that he must break
his vow to his father. The effect is beautifully managed, the
two currents meeting at the moment when Ushimatsu makes
his supreme effort and tells the truth. What can the ending
of the novel be, we wonder, as we approach the last few pages
with no solution in sight. It comes, a pure *deus ex machina*.
The *eta* who was driven from Ushimatsu's inn at the outset
of the novel reappears with an offer of a job on a ranch in
Texas, and Ushimatsu accepts, setting off with the young lady
who has remained faithful to him in spite of the awful truth
of his background. The ending vitiates the story for us, but
it was perhaps the only possible one for Japan. I think it likely
that in a European novel of the same date, it would be far

more usual that the hero, offered the choice of a comfortable job in Texas or badly paid work as a battler for *eta* rights in Japan, would have chosen the latter. In this the Japanese novel is realistic as European works are not.

The Broken Commandment is an example of one important result of European influence of Japanese literature, the increasing interest in social problems. On the whole Japanese poetry remained true to the old spirit, in spite of the innovations in the forms, but other branches of literature came increasingly to serve as vehicles for new thought. When we look at lists of European novels translated in the early years of Meiji, we are struck and perhaps amused by the preponderance of political novels, such as those of Disraeli or Bulwer Lytton, and in the works written under European influence this political element is equally conspicuous. The realism of such writers as Zola was, initially at least, not of great interest to the Japanese because many of the subjects which Zola treated were the most common themes of their own literature, and the realism with which he shocked Europe was quite matter-of-fact to the Japanese. The real challenge for them lay in the field of political and social writing, something quite new in their fiction. *The Broken Commandment* attempted to discuss the problem of the *eta* in such a way as to arouse sympathy for those unfortunate people, but always within the limits of an interesting story. Other attempts at social questions were usually more crudely done.

The concern with social problems showed itself most clearly in the adaptations of European works. For example, *A Fool's Love* (1925) by Tanizaki Junichirō seems to have been based on Maugham's *Of Human Bondage*. It tells of a man who falls in love with a waitress and lives with her for a time. Her essential coarseness often repels him, but he is so fascinated by her that even when she indulges in some particularly offensive vulgarities he can find ways to excuse her to himself. Eventually he discovers that she is unfaithful to him, attempts to break away but cannot. The novel ends with his abject surrender to her. He agrees that she can have whatever male friends she chooses, can live as she pleases, and need only remain as his wife. In Maugham's novel the emphasis was on the sensitive young man and his struggles to discover some way of surmounting a passion which completely possessed him. In Tanizaki's version of what is essentially the same story, the emphasis is rather on the terrible results of a fondness for Western things. What attracts the hero to the waitress is first of all her European features, which make him think of Mary Pickford's, and her curiously un-Japanese manners. When he asks her if she would like to go to the films, she replies in Mildred's words, "I don't mind if I do," instead of with the usual polite protestations. The hero is captivated by her unusual behaviour and encourages her to be modern—that is, European. This accentuates her naturally wayward inclinations. At the end of the novel, we find them married, living in a Western-style house, and his wife's new friends are European men.

Tanizaki's novel thus represents a rather subtle return to the didactic works so scorned by Tsubouchi. *Of Human Bondage* does not, as far as I am aware, seek to impart any moral lesson, but contents itself with describing a hopeless love-affair and its eventual resolution. But in Tanizaki the hero is condemned for his adulation of the West. He is represented as being ashamed of his shortness, dark complexion, protruding teeth— all typically Japanese features. He feels it somehow an honour even to be insulted by his European-looking mistress, and the thought that he possesses her fills him with pride, even when he sees her coarsely made up, and looking for all the world like a Eurasian prostitute. Undoubtedly a feeling of racial inferiority existed and still exists in Japan, and Tanizaki's novel was an attempt to combat it, rather than a simple description. His characters, when compared with those in *Of Human Bondage*, lack complexity and depth, but this is true, as I have indicated, of almost all Japanese literary personages.

Problems of another sort were treated by writers of the so-called proletarian literature, who flourished especially in the 1920's. The most famous work of this school of writing was *The Crab-Canning Boat* (1929), by Kobayashi Takiji (1903–33). This is the account of a voyage to the coast of Kamchatka by a small combination fishing and canning boat fleet. There is very little plot, and no attempt at characterization, in *The Crab-Canning Boat*, but the descriptions of the conditions under which the men live are extremely vivid. Among the crew are some students, who are unaccustomed both to the disagreeable work and to the uncouth sailors among whom they live. The officers and petty officers of the ship are fiendish and take sadistic delight in inflicting punishment on the crew, especially the students. The company which sends them out is represented as an organization of monsters. When, then, the ship comes in contact with a party of charming Soviet subjects, and a Japanese-speaking Chinese communicates the glad tidings of Marxism, it spreads with powerful effect among the crew.

If the Communist propaganda in such works as *The Crab-Canning Boat* seems excessively crude, it should be remembered that it was about the same time that in America such works as Odets' *Waiting for Lefty* (1935) were written. This play features a scene in which a young man asks for bread and is given a copy of the Communist Manifesto which, he is told, is as necessary for his soul. Indeed, the similarities between almost any aspect of Japanese literature produced between 1900 and 1941 with works produced at the same time in Europe and America are such that to give a full account of the trends in Japanese literature during the period would necessitate an equally long study of the European trends to which they are intimately connected. This is not to say that Japanese literature lost its individuality, but it now assumed the shape of local or regional variations on the main stream of modern literature, and not, as earlier, of an entirely independent tradition. This was particularly true of the novels, somewhat less true of poetry where, in spite of vigorous new movements which followed on the heels of European *avant-garde* experiments, the traditional forms continued to exert a powerful attraction for writers. In the field of the drama, European methods were most frequently employed, even when the subjects were taken from medieval Japanese history.

The older genres of Japanese literature were not abandoned, however. The diary, for example, came back into its own as a popular literary medium with the publication of a series of war diaries by Hino Ashihei, which reflect the day-to-day life of a soldier during the so-called China Incidents in the 30's. The popularity of these works was such that no Japanese soldier or sailor would have dreamt of being without his diary, if only to record that it rained, or that he got up at six o'clock. But the diary was also used in the 30's for impressionistic reflections, as it was in earlier days. An example of this use of the diary is Hori Tatsuo's *The Wind Rises* (1938–9), a sensitive, poetic account of the death of his wife by a young writer. The diary form is typically Japanese, but there is more than one suggestion of Gide's *Symphonie Pastorale* in the method of narration. The work indeed represents a blending of native and foreign forms seldom so successfully achieved.

In the writings of the early Meiji period there was often

little to suggest that the author was aware of the Japanese literary traditions, and only inadvertently, as it were, does he betray in his use of imagery or in his descriptions the non-European aspects of his writings. But some writers continued deliberately to use the traditional styles, even when the subjects were dictated by the new tastes, and other writers who had at first gained celebrity for their works in the modern vein turned back to the old classics for inspiration. After Tanizaki had written *A Fool's Love*, with its condemnation of the mania for Western things, he himself began to show in his works a more active interest in traditional writing. This tendency culminated in 1938–41 with the publication of his modern-language translation of *The Tale of Genji*. During this period he began also to plan the writing of a novel which would bear the same relation to the present time as *The Tale of Genji* did to that of Lady Murasaki. But with the advent of war in 1941 and the adoption of increasingly repressive measures by the Japanese Government in an effort to eliminate all traces of what they considered to be decadent culture, *The Tale of Genji* itself fell into disfavour, and Tanizaki's projected novel had to be put aside.

During the war itself little literature of importance was published and the production after the war at first promised to be extremely sickly. In the terrible years of 1946 and 1947, when most of the people were forced to devote their entire energies to the one question of staying alive, there was little interest shown in literary production. Certain left-wing writers who had been imprisoned or exiled returned to write memoirs, and their books, together with translations of foreign works, especially American, took up a large part of the booksellers' lists. But of genuine literary production there was very little. Pornographic novels, detective stories, and other types of escapist

literature began to appear, reflecting the low standard of the
tastes of the reading public. One magazine publisher I know
of, in order to sell his monthly, was forced to put a nude figure
on the cover of each issue, and to disguise even the serious
stories with titles of a vaguely indecent nature.

This phase of post-war fiction was succeeded by that of the
war memoirs, not as in this country by famous generals and
admirals revealing how it all happened, for most of the top-
ranking Japanese officers were dead or imprisoned, but by
ordinary soldiers. Some of them had been captured by the
Americans and wrote of their experiences as prisoners. Others,
and these were more interesting, told of the return of the con-
querors of South-East Asia to the cold, miserable Japan of 1945.
One of the best of these books was by a woman, Hayashi
Fumiko (1904–51), and like an earlier novel by Futabatei Shimei
was entitled *The Drifting Cloud* (1951), this being a familiar
Japanese symbol for a person with no aims or occupation.
The book tells of a young woman who goes to Indo-China
to serve as a typist with the Japanese army of occupation. After
years of austerity life in Japan, the luxury and luxuriance of
Indo-China dazzles her, and under these exotic influences she
turns from a mousy little typist to a *femme fatale*. In a small
town in the hills behind Saigon she has a tempestuous love-
affair with one of the Japanese army employees. The intensity
of their love is perhaps increased by their feeling that, since
Japan was fated to lose the war, they must exhaust the possibility of happiness which each moment gave them. When the
war does end and they are repatriated, everything in Japan
seems mean and ugly. Their love is killed by the drab surroundings and the difficulty of earning a living. The man
returns for a time to his family and the woman has an affair
with an American soldier. The days pass monotonously and

meaninglessly, without pleasure and without hope of better. And it is always raining.

I can think of few gloomier books than The Drifting Cloud. As an evocation of the Japan of 1945–7 it was extremely successful, and in its tone it sometimes suggests the Japanese medieval accounts of the sorrows of this world. But such a book is too close to the facts which inspired it to permit any real literary quality.

Above the mass of Japanese post-war literature, with its cheap pornography and its masochistic recollections, stands one work to which I have several times referred already, Tanizaki's The Thin Snow. In Japan it has been acclaimed as a masterpiece, and perhaps it is one, of a kind, but to a Western reader it never quite comes off, although at its best it approaches greatness. As far as I am aware, Tanizaki has not divulged the theory which he was following when he wrote this work, but if one compares his monumental trilogy with, say, Jules Romains' Les Hommes de Bonne Volonté, one can see his methods quite clearly. Romains, in attempting to portray a whole society, rather than one or two individuals, declared his dissatisfaction with the usual methods employed in long novels—having an entirely unlikely number of events happening to the hero or perhaps to one or two families. He instead preferred to take a large number of people, some of whom will never know each other in the course of his work, because only in this way could a great variety of experiences be naturally furnished. Tanizaki's method is the exact opposite. He takes a few people and allots to them only the number of experiences which they could normally have been expected to have in the course of five years, which means of course that there is almost no plot. The Thin Snow is as exact a recreation of life as exists in fiction, and Tanizaki, in choosing so photographic an approach, deliberately sacrificed all dramatic possibilities. How great a change this represented from his earlier work may be seen when we recall that his reputation was built as a writer of gruesome stories, and his middle period deals chiefly with highly theatrical monomaniacs. In *The Thin Snow*, Tanizaki is at pains to make everything exactly and completely true to life. His naturalism does not consist merely in the presentation of commonplace or unattractive details, although the book does contain a remarkably complete account of an attack of dysentery ; Tanizaki sees to it that every dramatic moment is followed by its natural let-down, that the continuous movement of life is not interrupted by the ends of chapters. Here, then, is a true *roman fleuve*, a slow and turbid river of a book, which moves inevitably and meaninglessly to its close.

It is difficult to give even an outline of the plot of the novel, so rambling and diffuse is it. The central figures are four sisters, and the most important single theme is that of finding a husband for the third of these sisters. But *The Thin Snow* is not really a novel in which the plot is of great importance. It is an effort of memory to recreate what must have seemed to Tanizaki in 1947 to be a vanished world. Here we have a prosperous family living in the Japan of 1936–41, and Tanizaki lovingly recalls each detail of their lives, as some Roman historian might have done five years after the fall of Rome under the Barbarians. The people in the novel never go merely to a " restaurant ", but always to the " Oriental Grill " or some other specific place, and when they go to meet their friends or lovers, we are told the number of the bus that they take. At first the precision of Tanizaki's reporting is likely to puzzle us, for accustomed as we are to the Proustian method of sounding faintly *leitmotivs* that must be retained in our minds until the moment of their full development, we feel sure that there must be some reason, for example, why Dr. Kushida is carefully described as being abrupt and short-tempered. Perhaps, we think, there will be a future moment at which the doctor's abruptness will be the focal point of a great scene, but in so supposing we are mistaken. Tanizaki says that the doctor is abrupt because he *is* abrupt. When people in other novels fall ill, they are likely to die, or at least to reach the very brink of death, but in *The Thin Snow* people who are taken ill usually get better after a few days in bed. The effect of all this realism at the end of 1,400 pages is quite overpowering. We feel exactly as if we have lived with the family, and we are certain that we should instantly recognize any of its members if we met them again. I do not mean that we have any deep insights into the characters of the personages of the novel. Tanizaki does not claim any more knowledge of what they are really thinking than we should have had if we were living in the same house. If they smile on a sad occasion, we can infer that they do not mean it, but Tanizaki never informs us that the heroine's heart was really breaking. In fact, we feel more strongly in this work than any other that there may be an emotional blank behind the Japanese. The author keeps nothing from us—not the brand of the toothpaste they use, nor the frequency with which they go to the lavatory—but when the lover of the fourth sister dies, a man for whom she was prepared to sacrifice everything, we have not the slightest indication of what she felt. Perhaps, we may end up by thinking, she did not feel anything at all.

The manner of *The Thin Snow* may not appeal to many Western readers, but we cannot fail to be impressed by the grand lines along which Tanizaki has conceived his story. It may be that Japanese literature, as exemplified by this novel, is entering a new period—one in which European influences have finally been absorbed into the native traditions, and techniques evolved with which we are as yet unfamiliar. The level of accomplishment of Japanese writers can now compare with that of any country, and as there is every likelihood that it will continue to improve, it may well happen that Japan, which has produced *The Tale of Genji*, the *Nō* plays, and other works of remarkable beauty, will again add to that small body of immortal works which belong not only to herself but to the entire world.

SELECTED BIBLIOGRAPHY

General Works

Aston, W. G.   *A History of Japanese Literature*, London, 1899.
Florenz, Karl.   *Geschichte der japanischen Litteratur*, Leipzig, 1906.
Revon, Michel.   *Anthologie de la littérature japonaise*, Paris, 1910.
Sansom, G. B.   *Japan ; A Short Cultural History*, London, 1931.
   The Western World and Japan, London, 1950.

Poetry

Bonneau, Georges.   *Anthologie de la poésie japonaise*, Paris, 1935.
Chamberlain, B. H.   *The Classical Poetry of the Japanese*, London, 1880.
Henderson, H. G.   *The Bamboo Broom*, Boston, 1934.
Manyōshū, published by Nippon Gakujutsu Shinkōkai, Tokyo, 1940.
Miyamori, Asatarō.   *Anthology of Haiku*, Tokyo, 1932.
   Masterpieces of Japanese Poetry, Tokyo, 1936.
Waley, Arthur.   *Japanese Poetry*, Oxford, 1919.

Theatre

Bowers, Faubion.   *The Japanese Theatre*, New York, 1952.
Iacovleff, A., and Elisséeff, S.   *Le théâtre japonais*, Paris, 1933.
Keene, Donald.   *The Battles of Coxinga*, London, 1951.
Peri, Noel.   *Cinq Nō*, Paris, 1921.
Waley, Arthur.   *The Nō Plays of Japan*, Grove Press, New York, 1953.

Novels and Other Prose

Omori, A. S., and Doi, K.   *Diaries of Court Ladies*, Tokyo, 1935.
Porter, W. N.   *The Tosa Diary*, London, 1912.
Sansom, G. B.   "The Tsuredzure Gusa," in *Transactions of the Asiatic Society of Japan*, Vol. 39, Tokyo, 1911.
Waley, Arthur.   *The Pillow-book of Sei Shōnagon*, Grove Press, New York, 1953.
   The Real Tripitaka, London, 1952.
   The Tale of Genji (one-volume edition), London, 1935.

Modern Japanese Literature and the West

Elisséev, Serge. *Neuf nouvelles japonaises*, Paris, 1924.

Futabatei Shimei. *An Adopted Husband*, New York, 1919.

Hino Ashihei. *War and Soldier*, London, 1940.

Hughes, Glenn. *Imagism and the Imagists*, Stanford, 1931.

Matsuo, K., and Steinilber-Oberlin. *Anthologie des poètes japonais contemporains*, Paris, 1939.

Natsume Sōseki. *Botchan*, Tokyo, 1924.

    La porte, Paris, 1927.

Yeats, W. B., and Pound, Ezra. *Certain Noble Plays of Japan*, Dundrum, 1916.

INDEX